Crushed Dreams: A Workers' Compensation Nightmare

Donna Scroggins

Dedication	3
Chapter 1	5
Chapter 2	9
Chapter 3	13
Chapter 4	21
Chapter 5	27
Chapter 6	31
Chapter 7	37
Chapter 8	39
Chapter 9	45
Chapter 10	51
Chapter 11	57
Chapter 12	61
Chapter 13	67
Chapter 14	71
Chapter 15	75
Chapter 16	79
Chapter 17	85
Chapter 18	93
Chapter 19	101
Chapter 20	107
Chapter 21	113
Chapter 22	125
Chapter 23	133
Chapter 24	139
Chapter 25	145
Chapter 26	149
Chapter 27	155
Chapter 28	161
Chapter 29	165

Chapter 30..167
Chapter 31..171
Chapter 32..177
Chapter 33..183
Chapter 34..187
Chapter 35..191

Dedication

This book is dedicated to my husband, the love of my life, who has suffered greatly due to another person's actions and the delays and denials of treatment by Workers' Compensation.

I am deeply sorry for the ordeal you have endured and continue to endure.

I am profoundly grateful that you are still here, being a loving husband, a caring father, and a wonderful grandfather. However, it saddens me to see you live your day-to-day life in such pain.

This book is also dedicated to all injured workers who have been hurt on the job and treated unfairly.

Your voices are being heard. I empathize with your pain and struggle. I understand the long, hard journey towards healing

Crushed Dreams: A Workers' Compensation Nightmare

and your fight with Workers' Compensation to obtain the desperately needed treatment.

This memoir reflects the author's current recollections of experiences over time.

Some names and characteristics have been altered.

Chapter 1

With the American dream becoming increasingly elusive and families facing greater struggles every day, we were thankful for our many blessings. Our small family was simply trying to live our best life. Unfortunately, the actions of another person drastically changed our lives that October day.

The year 2018 began with a series of unexpected events that forever altered the course of our family's life.

My husband and I were high school sweethearts; we dated throughout high school and, after graduation, got married in December 1990.

We welcomed our first son, Josh, in 1992. The first child is always the one you learn with. Josh was very smart, handsome, and challenging.

Crushed Dreams: A Workers' Compensation Nightmare

I certainly needed the patience of a saint with him. Our second child, a daughter named Ashley, was born in 1995. She was our first redhead, quiet, beautiful, sweet, sensitive, and quick in everything she did. She was such a well-behaved child, rarely needing correction. Then came our third child, another daughter, Autumn, in 1996. She, too, was a beautiful redhead.

Autumn was born with a port-wine birthmark and underwent about five years of treatment as she grew up. She was always brave, never complaining about the treatments, and showed amazing strength and courage. In 1998, our fourth child, a strong-willed, blonde-haired beauty named Alicia, arrived. Her strength and determination were astounding. She was a go-getter, always keeping us on our toes. Finally, our fifth child, a son named Zachary, was born in 2000. He, another handsome redhead, was sweet, sensitive, always eager to help, and brought immense joy, completing our beautiful family.

My husband and I have always been incredibly proud of our children; they have been such a blessing. We planned and wanted them close in age. We were blessed with smart, well-behaved, and beautiful children, and we have always been grateful for each of them.

My husband started working as a heavy equipment mechanic shortly after graduating. It was a natural talent for him. He was often told by friends and co-workers that he was the best mechanic around – the go-to man for a reliable fix. His mechanical talent was like none I had ever seen. Being mechanically inclined was definitely his God-given talent.

I would describe my husband as a caring, family man who worked very hard for his family, always striving to provide what he never had. He was motivated and diligent in his efforts to provide for us. Whether he had a doctor's or dentist appointment, he would schedule it early in the morning to avoid missing work. He rarely took sick days; if he did, you knew he must be very ill.

There are many good men and women who get up every day and work hard for their families. Unfortunately, these hard-working individuals are not always adequately protected in the workforce.

Before we had children, I worked as a dental assistant – my days before diapers. After our children arrived, my husband became the sole provider, and I became a stay-at-home mom, cherishing every moment of their lives. I couldn't have imagined it any other way.

My husband worked extremely hard in his career to provide for our family, and he was an excellent provider. We were an average middle-class family; our needs were always met, and he did an awesome job fulfilling most of our wants, which was a blessing.

Tracy attended many service schools over the years and rapidly advanced in his career. He worked long and hard to become the mechanic he was, frequently receiving job offers from various companies. It's amazing how companies advertise for experienced mechanics, offering "excellent pay," yet often the compensation does not match the required experience. A great mechanic can save a company significant money, and their pay should reflect that. My husband was a true mechanic, skilled in all aspects of his trade, not just specializing in one area.

You need a passion for the job, mechanical inclination, and love for what you do to excel as a mechanic. My husband once worked for an employer who, despite being very book-smart about engines, admitted he couldn't assemble one. He was one of the best employers my husband had worked for.

When my husband worked somewhere, he gave his all to the job, preferring to do everything in-house to save money for the employer. I have always been incredibly proud of him and his strong work ethic. It's fulfilling to love the work you do.

Life was going extremely well for our family. We had wonderful children, adorable granddaughters, and were in good health. We had more than some and less than others, and God blessed us with many great things in our life. We had a comfortable life until 2018 came roaring in like a lion, attacking the very core of our existence – mentally, physically, emotionally, and financially. Just when we thought it couldn't get worse, it did.

Chapter 2

2018 was one of the most challenging years of our adult lives, a year we wish had never come. The subsequent years tested our faith and resilience as a couple; it was a difficult path I wouldn't wish on anyone.

The year began like any other, ringing in the New Year at home, filled with optimism. Initially, everything seemed normal. In early February, our daughter Autumn had a quaint wedding at our home, attended by our family and that of her soon-to-be husband, Alec. It was a joyous day, celebrating your child finding the love of their life. Alec became our second wonderful son-in-law, joining Chris, who married our daughter Ashley three years earlier in a beautiful camouflage-themed wedding.

We were overjoyed that our daughters had found their soulmates. We also cherished our two granddaughters, one from Josh and the other from Ashley and Chris. The love and joy a grandchild brings is unparalleled – a true blessing.

Crushed Dreams: A Workers' Compensation Nightmare

We were ecstatic about our family's expansion and felt fortunate in life. However, life's tides began to turn, and there was no going back to the cozy life we once knew. How often do we take good times for granted, not considering bad times? Many people's lives change in an instant.

Just when we thought we had faced the worst, another problem emerged. The saying goes, "God doesn't give you more than you can handle," but those who say it often aren't in your shoes. After our experiences, I questioned that saying. The upcoming events were more than any family should bear.

Some days were overwhelming. I often found myself driving somewhere just to sit in my car and cry, questioning "Why, Lord?" But then, I'd remind myself to be strong, to talk to God for help because I couldn't do it alone.

I longed for things to return to how they were. I prayed for strength and, indeed, found more within myself than I ever knew existed. Difficult times reveal our true strength.

I had always relied on my husband to be the strong one, but now it was my turn to be strong for both of us. Perhaps "what doesn't kill you makes you stronger" was more apt for our situation. Our faith in the Lord's guidance was our rock. I often wondered how those without faith cope in such times.

Fear was a constant companion. How would we manage? I had left my career to raise our children, and Tracy had been the sole provider. As we aged, the invincibility of youth faded, replaced by the reality of life's fragility.

Our savings, including a fund for our granddaughters, dwindled quickly during tough times. Yet, even at our lowest, the Lord always provided. Just when I was close to losing hope, He came through, reinforcing the importance of unwavering faith.

This period was no different. I had to find faith, even as small as a mustard seed, that He would provide a way once again.

In the hardest times, don't lose faith. When you're in the valley, the mountain is on the horizon. This is our story, what we endured as individuals, a couple, and a family.

Chapter 3

At the end of February 2018, I went to see our family dentist. We had been living in another state and used the same dentist I had as a child, but after moving, we needed to find a new one. Our family had been going to this dentist for nine years. I thought he was a good dentist; in fact, I had been very picky because I used to be a dental assistant. When we first moved to this state, we changed dentists three times, as I looked for specific qualities in a family dentist. The three previous dentists just weren't what I was looking for, but we eventually found this dentist, who seemed to be just what we were looking for.

    I went in to have two crowns done. We have always taken good care of our whole family's teeth. My husband and I were getting older, and each of us had gotten a couple of crowns on our back molars. I had had crowns previously, so I thought it would be no big deal.

Crushed Dreams: A Workers' Compensation Nightmare

Never underestimate something so simple. I had always had good experiences with the dentist and never had a fear of them. The dental hygienist came in and gave me injections of Lidocaine. Immediately, something was different from any other time I had received an injection; this time, it hurt. My heart started racing and pounding; I found it hard to breathe and felt really sick to my stomach. My jaw started feeling unusual, with instant shooting pain, and I just felt overall unwell. My head hurt, and I could hear a ringing in my ear.

The hygienist gave me a couple more injections. I raised my hand up onto my chest and told the dental assistant I wasn't feeling well and needed to sit up for a few minutes. I explained to the assistant how bad I was feeling: my heart was still racing and pounding, and I was lightheaded. After sitting up for about ten minutes, I finally started feeling a little better, so the dentist came in and began working on the crowns. Once the crowns were done, he slowly sat me up in the chair.

Immediately, I felt sick to my stomach and went to the sink, feeling like I had to throw up. I told the dental assistant, "I really don't feel well at all, and my head hurts badly." I felt dizzy and sat back down in the chair for a few minutes. Finally, I stood up, stumbled to the bathroom, and noticed in the mirror that my face looked droopy on my left side. I tilted my head, thinking, "Usually it feels droopy, but doesn't look droopy."

As I walked past the receptionist, she said, "Bye, Donna."

It felt like she was far away, whispering my name, as if I was in a tunnel hearing her speak. It was quite unusual. I put my hand up and waved at her, then hurried to my car. As I walked, I felt strange, as if I was moving extremely slowly and things seemed out of place. I felt confused and had a major headache. I got in my car, shut the door, and sat there for a few moments, looking around, unsure if I could drive. I decided to call my husband and tell him how bad I was feeling and that I wasn't sure if driving home was a good idea. Maybe one of the kids could come get me.

I called my husband and said, "I'm out of the dentist and in my car. My face is droopy. It doesn't just feel droopy; it actually looks droopy, and my head hurts really bad."

As I went to tell him I didn't feel good, all I could say was, "I, I, I…"

I could hear the panic in his voice as he asked, "Donna, are you okay?"

I heard him talking to someone else on his work phone while on his personal phone with me. He yelled into his phone, "Hey, Donna is in the parking lot; I think she's having a stroke," his voice fading again, as if he was in a tunnel, "She's in a gold SUV. Yes, out there in your parking lot. She never left. You need to get out there!"

I was crying, confused. Was I having a stroke? Then I saw the dentist, dental assistant, and receptionist running out to my car. The dentist flung open my car door. By now, I had lost my speech. He said, "Go get the handheld blood pressure monitor."

The dental assistant ran back to the office, grabbed a digital blood pressure monitor, and ran back out to the parking lot. I heard the dentist say, "Her blood pressure is 80/60; she needs an ambulance NOW! Go call 911."

My blood pressure had always been around 116 to 120 over 70 to 72.

The dentist asked me to squeeze his hands, which I did.

He said, "You are not having a stroke, but you do have some Bell's Palsy going on." He kept reassuring me, "Donna, it's going to be alright."

The hospital was only two blocks away, so the ambulance arrived quickly. In the ambulance, I was a bit confused. The paramedic asked if I knew my birthday; it took a few minutes, but I was able to indicate the month and date with my fingers.

I arrived at the hospital and had no speech for three hours. After three hours, my speech slowly returned, my headache subsided, and I began to feel better. As my speech improved, my facial condition started to improve as well. They ran tests, took blood, and did all the necessary examinations.

The doctor at the hospital believed a nerve had been pricked. Bloodwork revealed I had a toxic overdose of lidocaine. I had a numb tongue, numb lip, and could not smell out of my left nostril. The next day, I had a lump in my jaw the size of a pecan. It was very painful. I went back to the dentist, who confirmed there was no abscess. It was just where my nerve had been pricked. I went for three days in a row and received an antibiotic shot in my buttocks each day. I'm not going to lie, it hurt.

We had been using this dentist for nine years. Initially, he was quite nice about the whole incident, but three to four weeks later, I contacted him to explain that I had incurred nearly $5,000 in medical bills due to the ambulance and ER visit, resulting from a toxic overdose and a pricked nerve. This was the amount after my co-pay and deductible.

He asked what I expected him to do about it, saying, "I don't have insurance to cover those medical bills. You don't expect me to pay for them, do you?"

I responded, "We have been coming to you for nine years. I came in for two crowns, left in an ambulance, and now I have almost $5,000 in medical bills, and you won't cover it?"

He replied, "No, I won't."

It was his dental hygienist who pricked my nerve and gave me the toxic overdose. I went to the courthouse and filed a case in small claims court, providing the court with his office address, as I didn't know his personal one. A couple of days later, the dentist called me, cursing, "Well, I guess I can add being served at my office and being F****** sued to my list of things."

I hung up, unwilling to listen to that. I planned to present everything the hospital gave me to the small claims judge and let him decide if the dentist was liable.

I told my husband what happened. I didn't want to go to small claims court, but I also didn't think I should have to pay for these medical bills. My husband called the dentist and told him, "Do not call my wife and curse at her again. Shame on you! Our

Crushed Dreams: A Workers' Compensation Nightmare

family has been your patients for nine years. Aren't you supposed to have insurance for situations like this?"

The dentist hung up on my husband.

The next day, the dentist kept calling my phone. I didn't answer. He left a message asking me to call him back, but I didn't. He called my husband's phone and said, "My insurance company will pay the medical bills. Please ask your wife to call me. I apologize; I'm sorry for how I reacted yesterday."

I did call him back. He apologized for his behavior the day before and asked me to come to his office. That afternoon, I brought the actual bills and my ER discharge papers for him to see. He wrote a check to cover the hospital bills, saying his insurance would reimburse him. Then he said, "Just so you know, I have been talking with my colleagues, and they said that you would have to be 1 in 250,000 to get a toxic overdose from the amount of lidocaine I gave you."

"Well," I replied, "I guess I'm 1 in 250,000 then. Lucky me!"

I then went down and canceled the small claims case against him. I didn't want it to be like that, but that was the last time any of our family members went to that dentist. Our family of seven, my niece's family of five, and my other niece's family of three all found new dentists. We decided it was best to switch to a new dentist, as we just didn't feel comfortable going to him anymore.

We found a wonderful dentist who was very understanding about what happened and how I felt. I have had dental work with our new dentist and no problems whatsoever. I requested that only the dentist give injections, as I feel more comfortable with that, even though hygienists can give injections in our state.

In April, I went to an ENT because I had not regained my sense of smell or feeling in my lip or tongue. The ENT said, "I don't know how long it will take to get the feeling back in your lip or tongue, or if you will ever get it back. Only time will tell."

May came, and still, there was no feeling in my lip or tongue. In early June, I finally started getting my sense of smell back. Gradually, over the next month, into July, the tingling and numbness in my lip and tongue began to decrease, and eventually, I fully recovered.

We thought things were getting back to normal. We celebrated the 4th at our place with a spectacular firework display and cookout with the family. We had a wonderful 4th of July, and then celebrated my birthday. But in the third week of July, our oldest son started getting sick.

He had gone to work that day and came home ill, so he went to the hospital. The emergency room doctor told him he had heat exhaustion and dehydration. They gave him IV fluids and sent him home. The hospital had checked his heart enzymes, which were over 700, but we didn't find that out until a few days later. The ER never told him about his elevated heart enzymes.

He had suffered from viral cardiomyopathy at 18 and took over nine months to recover.

The next day, feeling even worse, he went to a different hospital. He informed them of his previous condition and what the other hospital had said. They ran his heart enzymes, which were now at 940, and he was airlifted to a larger hospital with stiffening of the heart.

Josh was in ICU for three days. I had been out of town, and my husband, who worked four hours from home, stayed at his apartment during the week and only came home on weekends. Sometimes I would join him for a few days. I rushed to the hospital to be with Josh.

The doctor said his heart was very sick and they would try a new medication. If it didn't work, our son would need a heart transplant. The medication was expensive, over $2,000 a month, but thankfully his insurance paid for it. With many prayers and the new medication, Josh immediately started seeing improvements in his heart.

He still has days where he is very sick and sometimes misses work, but we are thankful he is better. His road to recovery is going in a positive direction. The hospital he went to the night before should have recognized that with elevated heart enzymes and a previous heart condition, it could be something serious with his heart.

We were very thankful for all the prayers for our son and that he was at least getting better. What a year so far, and we were exhausted, with the year only half over.

Chapter 4

In early August, our youngest daughter, our fourth child, Alicia, noticed that she had what looked like little flat moles or freckles appearing on her legs. She pulled out some pictures from the previous year and saw that these freckles or moles weren't there before. She asked me, "Do you think that is unusual?"

I replied, "A little, maybe we should have a dermatologist look at them, just to be sure."

So, I called and made an appointment with a dermatologist.

I accompanied my daughter to her appointment, which started on a positive note. The dermatologist was smiling and making small talk. Alicia and I were giggling as the doctor examined the moles or freckles on her arms, saying, "Those look fine."

The doctor looked at some on her back and said, "Those look fine," but when she looked at the ones on her legs, her smile disappeared, and she had a puzzled look on her face.

She said, "Those are not moles."

The dermatologist then said, "I am going to do a biopsy, and you will get the results in a few days."

A bit alarmed, I asked, "Is something wrong?"

She responded, "Let's just wait for the biopsy to come back."

Despite her reassurances, her face expressed concern. I asked again, "Should we be worried?"

Once more, she said, "Let's just wait and see what the biopsy says."

The biopsy results came back quickly, just two days later. Our daughter was diagnosed with Systemic Mastocytosis. My daughter called me, crying, after she received the call. My heart sank. I had never heard of it but looked it up on the internet. I was devastated and heartbroken for her. All our family could do was pray for her and put it in God's hands.

Even when your adult children are grown, you never stop thinking of them as your child. She was an adult, but my heart ached, feeling sad for her. She will always be one of my babies. Systemic Mastocytosis is a rare blood disorder that occurs when the body produces abnormal mast cells that multiply. Mast cells defend against intruders such as allergens. In Systemic Mastocytosis, these abnormal cells trigger continuous allergic responses and multiply uncontrollably, affecting the skin and internal organs.

People with mastocytosis are susceptible to a variety of symptoms, including itching, hives, and anaphylactic shock caused by the release of histamine and other pro-inflammatory substances from mast cells. When mast cells undergo degranulation, the released substances can cause a range of symptoms that can vary in intensity.

The symptoms of mastocytosis often resemble those of an allergic reaction and may include, but are not limited to:

- Fatigue

- Skin lesions

- Darier's sign a reaction to stroking or scratching of urticaria lesions.

- Abdominal discomfort

- Nausea and vomiting

- Diarrhea

- Olfactive intolerance

- Ear/nose/throat inflammation

- Anaphylaxis shock from allergic or immune causes)

- Episodes of very low blood pressure (including shock) and faintness

- Bone and/or muscle pain

- Decreased bone density or increased bone density (Osteoporosis or Osteosclerosis

- Headache

- Depression

- Ocular discomfort

- Increased stomach acid production causing peptic ulcers (increased stimulation of Enterochromaffin cell direct histamine stimulation

- Malabsorption (due to inactivation of pancreatic enzymes by   increased acid

Our daughter was referred to a cancer center. Unfortunately, there is no Mastocytosis specialist in our state. We hope that raising awareness about Mastocytosis will help bring specialists to our state and every state. People with this diagnosis really need proper care, and each state should have at least one or two specialists.

I couldn't believe this was happening. Maybe I was in disbelief, thinking if I didn't believe it, it wouldn't be so. Regardless of how much we wished it wasn't true, it definitely was. Why was our family being hit so hard, first with our son and now our daughter?

Our daughter is an upbeat, positive person and hasn't let her diagnosis keep her from accomplishing anything. She is a strong, beautiful woman, always a wonderful person with a big heart. It seemed so unfair that this was happening to such a positive, lovely young lady. She has always been strong and independent. All our children have been such a special blessing in our lives. It felt so unfair, but what parent or individual doesn't feel that way when diagnosed? I think they always ask, "Why me, Lord?" I don't know why, but all you can do is trust that the Lord will watch over, care for, and protect you.

My heart was so emotional, and I was distraught. I started praying for our daughter multiple times a day. I have always prayed for our children, but I found myself in deep conversation with the Lord more lately. We are thankful for the many people who prayed for her and continue to pray for her. Continued prayers are and will always be welcomed. Prayers for all people with Mastocytosis, and for any family dealing with any kind of sickness. The best thing you can do for the people you love is pray for them.

Chapter 5

After July and August, we just didn't think our family could take any more. That's what one would think, and that's certainly what we were thinking. Surely, this bad mojo needed to leave. We did receive some good news: our second child, our daughter, and her husband were adding to their family. We were very excited that our third grandchild would be arriving in June 2019. Our daughter and son-in-law already had a beautiful daughter, our sweet granddaughter Kimber, and were hoping for a boy to complete their family. They wanted a healthy baby, of course, but since they were only planning on having two children, they were hoping for one of each. We needed some happy news, but the brief good news was just that—brief.

I think the rotten devil had only gotten started. He was right back at work, and this time, it was my turn again. In September, I was out brush hogging some trails on our property. I got off the tractor to move a log out of the way. I bent down to pick up the heavy log and somehow lost my balance, falling backward onto the wheel sticking up on the brush hog. Initially, I didn't realize anything was wrong. I pulled myself up to a standing position but immediately fell back to the ground. Stunned as to why I fell again, I looked down at my ankle, and it was dislocated, sideways. Oh my, I just knew it was broken. I couldn't walk and had forgotten my phone at the house, so I dragged myself back to the tractor and drove like a mad woman to the house, adrenaline pumping.

When I got to the back porch, I was yelling for help, but no one in the house could hear me. I drove the tractor around to the front, where I could see my two youngest children through the window, playing video games. I continued to yell and finally caught their attention. They thought I was yelling, "I got bit by a snake!"

My son and daughter ran out, yelling back, "How did you get bit by a snake?"

I said, "I didn't, look," and showed them my ankle.

My son Zachary lifted me from the tractor, and I instructed him to take me to the car. My daughter Alicia drove me to the hospital. Halfway there, the pain started to kick in, and I told Alicia to hurry, as I was in real pain.

At the hospital, they took X-rays and told me my ankle was broken in a couple of places and needed to be set. The doctor set the foot while I was awake, with only a little sedative. It was extremely painful. After the first attempt failed, the doctor had to try again without any more pain medication. The second attempt was successful. The doctor wrapped it and said I would need to see an orthopedic doctor. I got an appointment the next day, and three days later, the surgeon operated on my left foot, inserting a plate and nine screws. I also had nerve damage. The doctor said the plate and screws would be permanent. It was very painful and swollen.

Getting around the house was so hard. My daughter Alicia was about to start a new job and had already put in her two weeks' notice before I got hurt. She informed them of my accident and decided to help me at home before starting her new job. Her old job was understanding and let her quit without finishing the two weeks. I was so grateful for her help during those first couple of weeks; I don't know how I would have managed without her.

Our daughter and son-in-law, who were expecting their baby, did a blood test that reveals the gender of the fetus at nine weeks. The big gender reveal showed a baby boy, completing their family. What joy—a baby boy, our first grandson. We were so excited for them and for us, thrilled at the prospect of a new grandchild.

On my husband's birthday, our other daughter, Autumn, our third child, announced that she and her husband were also expecting their first baby. We would be getting a fourth grandchild that year. What exciting news—two new grandchildren in the same year, within months of each other. We were so happy.

Four weeks out from my accident, we would once again face difficulties, and our whole life was about to change dramatically, and not in a good way.

Chapter 6

Life as we knew it would never be the same from this point on. My husband had just turned 49 years old that September. He had been a mechanic since he was nineteen, marking a 30-year career. That career would all change on that late autumn day. Just like that, life as we knew it was changed in the blink of an eye.

On Friday, October 26, 2018, the day started like any other. My husband Tracy was at his job, working hard as always. He had been employed with this company for twelve years, so it was just a typical workday, a regular Friday. Tracy had returned from his lunch break when he saw an employee struggling to unload a piece of equipment from a lowboy trailer. The employee was yelling and cussing, trying to unload the equipment. My husband approached and asked, "What are you doing? Do you know how to unload this piece of equipment?"

The employee replied sharply and rudely, "Yes!"

My husband said, "I'm the mechanic for this company. You're new, right?"

The employee snapped back, "Yeah."

He then started complaining about how the supervisor was sending him back out of town to another job site. He was frustrated about having to deliver equipment after just returning. He mentioned that he was told he would be home for a couple of days before going back and didn't want to go right back out of town, especially since it was the weekend. My husband explained, "I'm just the mechanic, and I don't have any control over that, but that's kind of what life is like with pipeline work. When they need a piece of equipment to start a job on Monday, it must be delivered. I can help you unload the equipment, if you want."

The employee agreed.

My husband got up on an old CAT D6 sideboom that needed to be unloaded, while the other employee got on a CAT 320 excavator. As they started unloading the equipment, the other employee hit the machine my husband was on. Tracy began to yell, "STOP, STOP!"

He signaled for the employee to stop, holding up a closed fist. He shouted, "I don't want to work with you. YOU DON'T KNOW WHAT YOU ARE DOING! I'm getting off!"

At this point, my husband was not hurt. He had got the other employee to stop. When my husband looked at him, the employee threw his hands up in the air, not touching the controls. There was no reason for the employee to touch the controls again. However, as my husband stood up to exit the equipment, the other employee did the unthinkable and hit the machine with such force that it broke the bolts, knocking the gas tank loose. My husband felt something heavy hit him, instantly crushing him. He heard a pop and snap, and pain surged through him. His knee was dislocated, his back and hip were in excruciating pain, and his ankle was also hurting. He couldn't move, trapped and pinned in the machine, which did not have ROPS (Roll Over Protection System), as older equipment is not required to have it.

Tracy started yelling for the employee to help him, but the employee just stood there, not assisting. Tracy kept yelling for help, and finally, after what seemed like an eternity and thinking he was going to die, he spotted his friend Kevin across the shop's driveway. Tracy yelled, "Kevin, Kevin, help me!"

Kevin eventually heard him and came running.

Kevin yelled at the other employee to help and then called 911, as he couldn't free Tracy. The firefighters and paramedics arrived and worked for nearly an hour to free my husband. The owner of the company showed up and watched as the first responders worked to free Tracy.

I know this because another employee bystander had picked up my husband's phone and was recording video of the scene. The owner spoke to my husband as they were loading him into the ambulance saying, "I will take care of you, don't worry about a thing."

The ambulance met a helicopter in a nearby field. Tracy was then airlifted to the hospital.

The accident happened around 1:00-1:10 pm. At around 2:55 pm, I received a call from my husband's number. Normally, Tracy would call around this time on Fridays to say he was heading home.

"Hey, Sexy, you headed home?"

Instead, a voice I didn't recognize spoke. "Are you Tracy's wife?"

Immediately, I felt a sinking feeling.

"I work with your husband, he was in a very bad accident and he is being airlifted, you need to get here immediately."

I had to know, "How bad is it?"

"It's bad."

I was at the store with my daughter Ashley, my elderly mother, and granddaughter. We hurried to the car and drove home. I dropped my mom off at her house, grabbed a bag with a couple of outfits, and headed to the hospital, a five-hour drive away.

I called all of our children. My daughter Autumn and her husband headed to the hospital but got into a minor fender bender on the way. Thankfully, they were okay. Alicia drove my car, Ashley and her husband also headed to the hospital, while my son stayed with his daughter, and my other son couldn't take off work as he had just started a new job.

On the way, the same employee called me again, now from his phone. He told me he had locked Tracy's phone in his service truck. I asked him about the accident, and he said he heard the supervisor claim Tracy had been in a hurry. I told the coworker that didn't sound like my husband at all. The employee said he didn't know what happened, as he wasn't there at the time of the accident. He had videotaped the rescue efforts, which were on my husband's phone, and suggested the footage might be important.

The question remained: How did this supervisor know what happened if only my husband and the employee who refused to help were there at the time, followed later by Kevin?

I really don't know why the employer who came to the scene didn't call immediately after my husband was loaded into the ambulance. Why didn't the employer have one of the office personnel call me and report my husband had been in a work accident?

Tracy didn't remember much from the helicopter ride. All he could think about was the pain, so much pain. He did remember the EMT saying, "We'll be at the hospital soon. Don't close your eyes. Don't go to sleep. Stay with me. You're going to be fine."

We are incredibly grateful to the firefighters, first responders, and EMTs who worked tirelessly to free my husband from this horrific accident and to Kevin for hearing my husband's calls for help. There is so much appreciation and love for our brave firefighters and EMT workers. God bless them for their service.

Chapter 7

Just using common sense, these four principles, if applied, may have prevented this accident:

1. Know How to Operate Heavy Equipment
It's essential for anyone operating heavy equipment to know how to work the controls. Employers have an obligation to hire qualified employees and ensure they are trained for the job they are hired to do. Common sense dictates that if you don't know how to operate heavy equipment, then don't. And if you don't have the common sense to realize that, then at least stop when told to in a dangerous situation and remain stopped until it's safe.

2. Rollover Protection Systems (ROPS)
Newer equipment is required to have ROPS, a structure intended to protect operators from injuries caused by vehicle overturns or rollovers. ROPS, like roll cages

in cars and trucks, maintain a space for the operator's body in the event of a rollover. Defined by regulatory agencies such as the US Occupational Safety and Health Administration, these structures must meet strength and energy absorption requirements. In cases of operator failure or, as in this incident, another employee's error, ROPS could possibly prevent accidents.

3. Reporting to OSHA
It's crucial to report work-related accidents that result in hospitalization or death. Employers are required to do this, but don't assume they will. If injured, contact OSHA as soon as possible to ensure the accident is reported. This helps in the investigation and maintains workplace safety. Ideally, hospitals receiving patients from work-related accidents should be mandated to report these incidents, holding employers accountable and ensuring safety compliance.

4. Safety Measures and Alertness on the Job Site
Following safety rules, using equipment properly, wearing safety protection, helping others, knowing how to operate equipment, staying alert, and refraining from substance use on the job are all vital. This accident was 100% preventable. If the other employee had remained stopped when instructed, my husband would not have been injured. Your actions can significantly impact your health and that of others. In this case, due to seemingly deliberate actions, my husband's life was changed forever. Everyone's goal should be to return home in the same good health they arrived at work in.

Chapter 8

We were now traveling to the hospital where my injured husband had been taken. After five hours of travel, we all arrived at the ER, where Tracy was still waiting. The emergency room doctor explained Tracy's injuries to me: he had a shattered femoral head, fractured in many places (the femoral head is the upper part of the thigh bone and such fractures are rare, usually associated with hip dislocations), a fractured rib, a crushed thigh, stomach injuries, a dislocated knee believed to have torn ligaments, an ankle fracture, and a back injury. He had numerous scrapes and bruises on his stomach, back, leg, thigh, and buttocks. His work phone, which had been in his back pocket, was cracked, and there was an indentation about a half-inch deep in his left buttock. These injuries were documented at the hospital on the date of the accident.

In the video recorded by the coworker, you can clearly hear EMTs calling in a back injury and lower extremity injuries, which would later be important. After almost five hours in the ER, Tracy

Crushed Dreams: A Workers' Compensation Nightmare

was finally taken to his room. It was after 9:00 pm. As we were all talking with my husband in his room, a nurse came in and told us that visiting hours were over and everyone had to leave. Despite driving over five hours and Tracy's condition (he had been crushed by heavy equipment), no exception was made.

Our children and their spouses, my brother-in-law and sister-in-law, said their goodbyes for the night and left for a hotel, planning to return in the morning. I stayed with my husband. About thirty minutes later, he woke up screaming from a nightmare, reliving the accident. He was in extreme pain, so I went to get the nurse. She administered morphine, but 30 minutes later, Tracy was still in severe pain. When I went to get the nurse again, she dismissively said it wasn't time for more medication and that he shouldn't be hurting.

An hour passed, and Tracy was still in agony. The nurse barely peeked in and reiterated that it wasn't time for more medication. It was frustrating; how could she know the extent of his pain? Then, thirty minutes later, I noticed Tracy's arm was double in size. I fetched a nurse, who realized the IV had blown. Tracy hadn't been receiving any pain medication because it wasn't going into his vein. Her bedside manner and lack of compassion were appalling.

Another nurse was called, and they finally got the IV in correctly. Tracy finally began receiving morphine and some relief from his pain. The other nurse commented on how lucky he was to be alive, and it was clear that he was also lucky I had checked on him.

That night, Tracy had a long and painful time. He kept waking up, screaming from nightmares about being crushed. We hardly slept at all. We were in a large room where I had a bed to sleep on, which was a relief, as my foot was swollen and painful from not being elevated during the five-hour ride. In my rush, I had forgotten my pain medication.

The next morning, our children returned to see their dad before heading home. His brother and sister-in-law also came by to visit before they had to return to their own children. Friends and family were calling, checking on Tracy's condition, and I tried to keep everyone updated.

We received a call from the Workers' Compensation nurse case worker, who said they had already spoken to the other employee. This employee admitted that he did not know how to work the controls, and they also needed a written statement from Tracy. The following day, Tracy's employer and his brother-in-law, who also worked at the company, visited the hospital.

Upon entering the room, Tracy's employer whispered to his brother-in-law, "Look, his wife is on crutches," to which the brother-in-law replied, "Yes, his wife got hurt a couple of weeks ago and had surgery."

The employer responded, "I didn't know that."

My husband had mentioned my injury to the brother-in-law at work, but the employer was unaware, showing a lack of interest in his employees' lives.

Earlier that morning, Tracy had received a candy basket from the company. While there, his employer commented on the basket, joking that Tracy should watch his weight. The brother-in-law pointed out that the company had sent the basket, prompting the employer to reiterate the weight comment.

The employer expressed regret about Tracy's accident but quickly began asking about his return to work. As Tracy was still affected by pain medication, I answered on his behalf. I explained the severity of his injuries, including the shattered femoral head and the focus on his hip. His employer suggested a hip replacement, assuming Tracy could return to work in two weeks. It was absurd to think that someone with such extensive injuries could recover that quickly. Tracy's left side had been crushed, and he was pinned for an hour. He had bruises all over, possible ligament damage in his knee, a fractured rib and ankle, and severe bruising on his left buttock from his phone in his back pocket.

At around 280 pounds, Tracy had some cushioning, which I believe protected him and perhaps even saved his life. I doubt a thinner man would have survived, but that's just my opinion. I'm sure God was watching over him that day.

The employer and brother-in-law stayed for about 30 minutes. I was not impressed with the employer's level of concern about my husband's health or his focus on when Tracy could return to work. The employer didn't seem concerned about how the accident happened at his workplace. While there, he never asked about the accident's circumstances, which I found unusual and peculiar. Wouldn't a company owner want to know what happened, especially directly from the injured employee? Even if he had asked the other employee, shouldn't he get both sides of the story? Typically, companies fill out an accident report, but how could he do so without asking Tracy? With only two people present at the accident, it would make sense to question both. If I owned a company, my first question would have been about how the accident occurred.

Chapter 9

Since my husband was the sole provider, when I got hurt, we knew we had a large deductible to cover. So, we decided he wouldn't take time off when I had my surgery because we would have hospital bills from my injury. Our health insurance at the time had a $6,000 deductible. Consequently, when I underwent my surgery, my daughter Alicia accompanied me. It saddened me that Tracy couldn't be there, but over the years, we've made many sacrifices because some employers don't give their employees time off for family emergencies.

My husband tolerated the downsides of his job, which I think many people nowadays do, especially when they need a good-paying job. They adopt a work ethic of just getting through the day to go home. Tracy was well-paid, but at this job, he never received more than one week of vacation. Other companies he worked for before offered incentives like two weeks of vacation after five years and three weeks after ten years.

Crushed Dreams: A Workers' Compensation Nightmare

I've always believed that companies should invest in good, loyal employees who stay and invest in the company. Tracy ended up not taking a vacation each year, saving his vacation days for holidays since there was no holiday pay at this company. He used these days for the two days off at Thanksgiving and the three days off during Christmas so his paycheck wouldn't be short. Every previous employer he had worked for provided holiday pay and paid sick days. I had never heard of companies not offering holiday pay before. This was the first employer my husband had worked for that didn't offer it.

Hardworking employees often build wealth for their employers. Why don't some employers understand that without good employees, a company wouldn't thrive? Benefits like holiday pay, sick days, and paid vacations used to be attractive selling points for employment. However, more and more, these incentives are disappearing or becoming things of the past. Many people are realizing this is becoming the "norm" with companies. They expect people to do the work of two or three people, often with fewer benefits and lower pay.

I think too many people have become consumed with greed, forgetting to do the right thing. The Golden Rule – "Do unto others as you would have them do unto you" – seems to be a concept from the 'good old days' our parents talked about. High standards, morals, and employers valuing their employees seem to be diminishing. It appears it's easier to pretend to be a good person than to actually show it.

When a breadwinner is injured on the job, little thought seems to go into how the employee's life or family will be affected.

The struggle and financial burden faced by a family when an employee is injured at work are often overlooked.

For the employee who hurt my husband, life continued as usual the next day. He woke up able to walk and work, unlike my husband who lay in a hospital bed in extreme pain, facing multiple injuries and surgeries. For this employee, nothing seemed different. He wasn't in trouble for his actions, which appeared deliberate. In other situations, causing harm on purpose could lead to prosecution for assault or even attempted murder. Yet, in this workplace incident, it seems you can disregard instructions, continue a dangerous action after being told to stop, and severely injure someone without consequence.

For the employer, life also went on as before. The employer continued to earn, with the option to replace a hurt employee, and business carried on as usual. The employer wasn't crushed, injured by an angry employee, trapped, or facing the multitude of challenges that Tracy now faced. It's sad that someone's life can be dramatically impacted and changed by another's actions, particularly actions that seemed deliberate.

The only person who suffered was my husband, who merely wanted to return home in the same healthy condition he arrived at work. His thirty-year career was changed in a split second, altered dramatically by someone else's actions. I personally believe, based on what my husband described, that the employee's actions were intentional. However, Workers' Compensation stated that the employee admitted to not knowing how to work the controls.

If the employee truly didn't know how to operate the equipment, did he lie to get the job? If he only claimed ignorance after the accident, was it to avoid trouble? If he genuinely didn't know, then where does the responsibility of the employer lie in ensuring their employees are qualified for the work they're hired to do? Were references checked? Was any training provided?

Regardless of his knowledge of the controls, he was told to stop and did so initially, indicating he understood the command. After being told, "You don't know what you are doing," there was no reason for him to resume operating the equipment. Whether he knew how to work the controls or not, common sense should have prevailed. Most people possess this basic sense, or is that yet another excuse – "he didn't have common sense"?

If someone is yelling, "STOP, STOP," the logical response is to stop and stay stopped. You don't need special training for that, just the ability to listen – a skill most learn in grade school. This leads to another question: if he wasn't using common sense, was he perhaps impaired by drugs or alcohol? Hindsight is always 20/20, but no one knows for sure.

My husband would often overlook the things he didn't like about his job, a common attitude among those supporting a family. The allure of good pay, essential for providing for a family in today's cost of living, often overshadows other job aspects. As the sole provider, he felt the pressure to ensure there was enough money. He gave his all at his job to bring home sufficient funds to provide a good life for his family. He poured his whole life into being a good husband, a good dad, and a reliable provider, ensuring we had a home, good food, and a nice vehicle. He did what so many men and women do out of love for their family: work hard.

There are many hardworking people like my husband, laboring in dangerous job sites with no protection from hazardous employees. Every year, many good men and women lose their lives or get severely hurt because of these perilous jobs. The Arkansas House of Representatives should see this as an eye-opener. How many hardworking individuals must lose their lives or suffer severe injuries before better, fairer, and more equitable laws for all injured workers are passed?

My husband needed a high-paying job, partly because we often needed extra money for our son, who had heart problems. When our son missed work or lost a job, sometimes due to employers discovering his heart condition, we needed to help him. High-paying jobs like my husband's allowed us to assist our son and still cover our bills.

Some might say we didn't need to help an adult child, but that's not how we view parenting. We believe in supporting our children, regardless of their age, especially when they face health issues beyond their control. Parenting styles vary, and that's okay, but for us, providing help when our children need it is a fundamental part of being a parent.

Years ago, employers cared more about their employees, offering good pay and benefits. However, times have changed, and not for the better. The American dream is slipping away from the younger generations. People are struggling, living paycheck to paycheck, and often even two paychecks aren't enough. The struggle is real for many families, and I know many can relate to this.

Crushed Dreams: A Workers' Compensation Nightmare

Young people are losing hope as the American dream, once within reach of our parents and grandparents, slips further away for the next generations. With inflation, wages don't match living costs, and taxation is heavy. Not all, but many employers don't care about their employees' well-being, viewing them as replaceable. Some companies rely on temporary agencies, never offering permanent employment or benefits.

It's time for us to seriously consider the current situation. If you were to get hurt at work due to another employee's actions, would you be protected under current Workers' Compensation laws? Sadly, the answer is likely "No."

Chapter 10

My husband has replayed the event over and over in his head, but what good does that do? You can't change an event that has already happened. He has said, "I should have never helped that employee that day," but that's not in line with his personality; he has always been someone who helps people. That's one of the traits I love about him – he has a kind heart. He would stop to help people broken down on the side of the road and always picked up hitchhikers, offering them a ride as far as he could take them. When we lived in another state, he would pick up homeless people and take them to shelters, even giving them a few dollars if he had any.

Tracy was always giving money to people with signs; he was just that kind of person with a big heart for others. For him to say, "I never should have helped him that day," doesn't change the kindness in his heart. Without hindsight, he would have naturally done what he's always done. So, that day, he would have still helped that employee, and the event that unfolded would have still occurred. The sequence of events for that day was already in motion.

Sometimes, bad things happen to good people. I believe all things happen for a reason, although we may not know the reason when they occur. What plan did God have for us? Was He going to use this accident for some greater good? Was there a purpose for why it happened? If so, we didn't know what that purpose was yet. Of course, I wish this accident had never happened, but only God knows why it did. Right now, we didn't have a clue why it happened, but it happened, and now we must deal with the hand that was dealt. The devil must have dealt this hand because it was a pretty crappy hand.

After his employer and brother-in-law left, I checked to see when Tracy's surgery was scheduled. I was told it might be later that day or maybe tomorrow. My leg was really swollen, and I asked if I could use a wheelchair to get to the cafeteria, as it was difficult to carry food on crutches. However, I was told "no," as wheelchairs were for patients only, even though there were three wheelchairs on that floor. As a result, I didn't make it to the cafeteria all day Saturday.

Tracy lay there in excruciating pain, having been crushed, with the uncertainty of whether his surgery would happen later that day or the next. I kept wishing they had taken my husband to a different hospital; I was unhappy with the treatment he was receiving and the nurses' rudeness. The denial of a wheelchair for me to get to the cafeteria seemed unnecessarily unkind. These nurses needed a lesson in compassion, as Ephesians 4:32 says, "Be kind and compassionate to one another, forgiving each other, just as in Christ God forgave you."

That night, we had another rude nurse. We told her about the previous night's blown IV and Tracy's severe pain, and her response was, "Just be thankful you are alive." We were thankful, but that didn't change the fact that Tracy was in pain and the nurses were not managing it well. If they had been doing their job properly, Tracy's pain would have been better controlled.

I was also grateful that Tracy survived to tell what really happened, as I wondered what the company would have said otherwise. The supervisor had a history of protecting the company at all costs. By spreading a story immediately, it seemed like they were covering their bases in case Tracy didn't make it. Other employees had heard this version of events from the supervisor, but Tracy corrected them, questioning how the supervisor knew what happened since he wasn't present.

Tracy often wondered if the employee who hurt him had been tested for drugs or alcohol, as his reaction to the accident was not normal. Normally, people help when someone is hurt, but this employee just stood there, not helping. It felt surreal, like a horror movie.

On Sunday morning, I asked about the surgery again, and the nurse said it was scheduled for that afternoon. Finally, around 2:00 pm, they came to take Tracy to surgery. At the hospital, I met a kind young man and explained my difficulty getting around on crutches. He kindly got me a wheelchair and advised me to hide it in our room when not using it, or the nurses would take it. His helpfulness was a stark contrast to the other staff we had encountered. Everyone else on my husband's floor had insisted that wheelchairs were strictly for patients, even though there were several available.

Finally, the doctor came to see me, and he definitely didn't look like a typical doctor. He was wearing cut-off jeans, a white t-shirt, cowboy boots, and a cowboy hat. In a skeptical, low voice, I asked him, "Are you the doctor?" He replied, "Yes, I am." Now, I have nothing against cut-off jeans, cowboy hats, and boots – in fact, cowboys can be quite sexy. However, I believe there's a time and place for everything. When I go to the beach, I wear beach attire. When I go to a rodeo, I wear rodeo attire. But when someone is coming to perform surgery, I'd prefer they didn't look like they were ready for eight seconds on a bull named Intimidator.

I asked, "How many times have you done this type of surgery, repairing a shattered femoral head?" He responded, "Never, this will be my first, but I have another doctor supervising me, so there's really nothing to worry about." I was taken aback and replied, "What?" The doctor explained that he had fixed many broken hips but never a broken femoral head. He mentioned that most patients with this injury from high-impact crashes are either dead on arrival or die shortly after. He hadn't performed this type of repair surgery before, but he knew how to do it.

I was apprehensive, to say the least. I always question when someone says, "You have nothing to worry about." It's like the famous saying, "I'm from the government, and I'm here to help." Yikes! Never be afraid to speak up and ask for a different doctor. Trust your gut instinct. The first thing I should have done when I arrived at this hospital, after the first night's interaction, was to request a transfer to another hospital. I would never willingly go to this hospital again. Our experience had been horrible – rude, unprofessional staff with terrible bedside manners and zero compassion.

If it were a life-or-death situation, I would only have them patch me up enough to get me to the next hospital. I regret not speaking up and advocating for my husband when he couldn't. We held hands and prayed for the doctor's hand to be guided by God's and for God to watch over Tracy during the surgery.

While Tracy was in surgery, I used the wheelchair to get something to eat, as I hadn't made it to the cafeteria the day before. It was much easier with the wheelchair. After eating, I returned and prayed some more, knowing that our family members and friends were praying as well.

Chapter 11

While Tracy was being operated on, I met a man who shared that he and his wife were team truck drivers and had been in a bad accident. He wasn't seriously hurt, just a few scratches and bruises, but his wife took the brunt of the impact. They were 14 hours from home, without clothes or a phone charger. His wife, injured on Friday, had broken a bone in her upper leg, and they were placing a rod through it. She had been left waiting since Friday, all of Saturday, and half of Sunday. He expressed his disappointment with their treatment, noting they too had been treated poorly. We found common ground in the fact that both our spouses were Workers' Compensation patients, leading us to wonder if such treatment was standard for all patients or just those on Workers' Compensation. We ended our chat wishing each other's spouses a speedy recovery and offering prayers.

Approximately two hours later, I was informed Tracy was out of surgery. The doctor briefly told me the surgery went as well as it could have and that Tracy would be non-weight bearing for at least 6 months or longer, depending on his healing process. I texted his employer to update them on his surgery and the six-month non-weight bearing prognosis. The employer simply replied, "Okay, thanks for letting us know."

When I was allowed to see Tracy in the recovery room, he was throwing up, having not handled the anesthesia well. The recovery room's cleanliness was concerning; it was dirty, with marks on the floor, dried blood, and a wet puddle that I hoped was just water. I worried about the risk of a staph infection in such conditions and hoped the operating room had been cleaner.

Upon returning to his room, I discovered our belongings were gone, and someone else was in his bed. I asked the nurses where Tracy's personal belongings were and why there was someone else in his room. They informed me they had moved him to a smaller room. This new room was so cramped that the closet door could only open about 5 inches, barely enough to reach in for something. With a curtain dividing Tracy's bed from the other patient, my chair was touching the railing of the other man's bed, making it uncomfortable and invasive.

The other patient, who had been drinking and crashed his motorcycle, was under police watch. He spent most of the night throwing up, yelling out profanities, and making it nearly impossible for Tracy to rest. The nurses did little to quiet him, simply closing the door. Now, with only a chair to sleep in, I was extremely uncomfortable.

Tracy kindly suggested I join him in his hospital bed, but given it was a single bed and he was swollen and in pain from surgery, I declined. "No, babe, I will be alright," I assured him, grateful for his offer but concerned about his comfort.

The next day, I again encountered the man from the truck accident, whose wife was also injured. He mentioned that when his wife returned from surgery, they had given their room to someone else. I shared that they had taken away my husband's room as well. He mentioned being 14 hours from home, while we were 5 hours away, and both of us only had chairs to sleep in.

I approached the nurses' station to inquire why people without overnight guests couldn't be placed in the smaller rooms, leaving the larger rooms with beds for those from out of state, like my husband and the other woman. Both of us, being Workers' Compensation patients and far from home, were struggling with tiny rooms and uncomfortable chairs for sleeping. The nurse's response was dismissive: "Can't help it."

I noticed a couple of larger rooms were vacant, so I returned to the nurses' station to ask if my husband could be moved. After speaking to the head nurse and explaining our situation, I was simply told, "No, you are in a room."

Frustrated, I went to the hospital administrator's office to complain about how my husband was being treated and the availability of larger rooms. They said they would look into it, but my complaint seemed to lead nowhere. In fact, after I complained, the nurses became even more rude to us.

The night was long and difficult. My brother had been killed by a drunk driver at 18, and we had to spend the night listening to a drunk driver in the next bed complain about his situation. It was upsetting to hear him blame others for his own actions, reflecting how no one seems to take responsibility these days. I found myself so upset by his constant complaining and foul language that I prayed for him to quiet down, even hoping for laryngitis – a horrible thought, I know, but I was exhausted, in pain, and frustrated. Unfortunately, my prayers went unanswered.

The drunk driver kept complaining, throwing up, and cursing at the nurses. He seemed to know no other words but curse words, and my husband, who was trying to rest after major surgery, struggled to get any sleep.

Chapter 12

The next day, my husband started telling me that something felt wrong with his hip. He mentioned a lump the size of a golf ball in his left buttock, which hadn't been there before the surgery. When the doctor visited the next day, my husband mentioned the lump, but the doctor looked puzzled and shrugged off the complaint, simply saying, "I don't know." It was concerning – if the doctor didn't know, then who would?

We asked about when his crushed leg and knee would be examined and evaluated further. The doctor said the hip was the main concern right now and that more x-rays would be taken sometime that day. The next day, they took him for more x-rays, but the doctor said they didn't see anything broken and suggested a possible MRI later to check for torn ligaments, as x-rays wouldn't show ligament damage. I was puzzled why they couldn't do an MRI while he was already in the hospital.

Crushed Dreams: A Workers' Compensation Nightmare

On Tuesday morning, I ran into the other Workers' Compensation truck driver in the cafeteria. He shared his struggles, including a two-mile walk to a hotel, and his efforts to purchase essentials like a charger and clothes. His wife was getting an ambulance ride home, arranged by Workers' Compensation, but he couldn't accompany her and was trying to get a flight. He expressed how this had been the worst experience of their lives. We exchanged Workers' Compensation carriers and found that, despite having different insurers, our experiences were strikingly similar. It seemed Workers' Compensation patients were treated poorly in general. He anticipated his wife's departure on Thursday, and we wished each other luck and prayers.

I didn't see the truck driver again during our stay. I often thought about them and prayed for his wife's healing. Their situation highlighted just how challenging dealing with Workers' Compensation could be. Every day was a struggle for my husband, still in immense pain, with his other injuries untreated. His back, stomach, leg, thigh, ankle, and now his hip with the lump, all caused him discomfort. It was baffling why the hospital didn't conduct an MRI on his knee, thigh area, and back while he was already admitted.

Tracy mentioned that the relief from the morphine shots lasted only about two hours, leaving him in pain and waiting for the next dose of medication. The first two hours provided relief, but then he was left hurting, highlighting the inefficiency in managing his pain.

The next day, I saw the man again whose wife was injured in the truck accident. He shared that after his wife's surgery, they had also lost their room. Like us, they were far from home and only had a chair to sleep in. I inquired at the nurses' station why those without overnight guests weren't placed in the smaller rooms, reserving larger rooms with beds for out-of-state patients like us and the truck driver's wife. The nurse was unhelpful, replying, "Can't help it." Seeing some larger rooms vacant, I asked for a room change, but even after speaking to the head nurse and hospital administrator, nothing was done, and the nurses became even ruder.

Friday marked a week since we'd arrived. I was out of clean clothes, in pain, and exhausted from sleeping in a chair. I decided to drive home for a night to get some rest and clean clothes. Tracy initially resisted, fearing worse treatment in my absence, but eventually agreed to leave with me. The hospital staff advised against it, stating he needed more treatment. However, his other injuries hadn't been addressed, and he now had a new lump in his hip.

As we prepared to leave, a nurse took away the wheelchair I had been using, seemingly annoyed at our decision to leave. It was a struggle to get to the car, which was parked two blocks away. Tracy was in immense pain, making the five-hour drive home excruciating for him. We barely made it to the pharmacy in time to fill his pain medication prescription, which was nearly denied due to a missing detail.

Finally home, our sons and son-in-law helped transfer Tracy inside amidst pouring rain. Every movement caused him unbearable pain. Despite the challenges of being home, it was a relief to be away from the hospital's negative environment. There's no place like home, especially after such a harrowing experience.

Crushed Dreams: A Workers' Compensation Nightmare

That night, my mind was occupied with thoughts of the upcoming tasks needed to make Tracy's life at home more comfortable. He still required treatment for his back, his stomach was hurting, his knee needed attention, and his thigh was in excruciating pain from being crushed. He also had a fractured rib and ankle. The pain pills were not effectively controlling his pain. Even the morphine provided relief for only two hours before wearing off.

A couple of days later, we met with the Workers' Compensation nurse case worker at a doctor's appointment. Getting Tracy to his first appointment was a challenge. We expressed our lack of necessary supplies, and she assured us she would be obtaining them for us. During the appointment, we mentioned to the doctor that Tracy's leg hadn't been examined. His response was, "That's the least of your worries."

It was disheartening to hear that other injuries wouldn't be addressed because another injury was worse.

The wheelchair we eventually received was the same size as the one we borrowed – a standard model. I pointed out to the Workers' Compensation nurse that, although Tracy could fit into the wheelchair, it was tight and uncomfortable due to his swollen hip. I requested a 22-inch wheelchair for more comfort, but the nurse denied this, stating that if he could fit into the current one, that was all Workers' Compensation would provide. This attitude was frustrating. Just because Tracy could fit into the wheelchair didn't mean it was the right size, especially with his severe swelling making it painful and uncomfortable. It seemed like the bare minimum was all we could expect, with little effort made to ensure his comfort during healing.

Tracy continually complained about his back, knee, and thigh at every appointment. His stomach also hurt for the first two to three weeks, bruised from the crushing injury, and urinating was painful during this time. Finally, after another week, he received an ankle brace for his fracture and a knee brace to stabilize his knee.

I sent text messages to his Workers' Compensation case worker nurse, stressing that Tracy's other injuries hadn't been evaluated or treated and asking when they would be looked at by a doctor. Tracy relayed his back pain and need for treatment to his home health nurse, who said she would document it in her notes. However, it felt like his health wasn't a priority and his requests for treatment were being ignored.

Chapter 13

On November 7, 2018, I sent a text message to the Workers' Compensation nurse, expressing concerns about Tracy's stomach and back pain and asking when he would receive treatment for his back. Her response was always to "just mention it at the next appointment." However, this advice felt futile as Tracy had been mentioning it at every appointment, yet nothing was being done. It seemed as though they were hoping the problem would somehow resolve itself if ignored. The approach appeared to be focused on getting him back to work as soon as possible, regardless of his health status.

Injuries don't just disappear without treatment; in fact, without proper care, how was Workers' Compensation expecting him to improve? Delayed treatment is detrimental to health, and it's unreasonable to expect someone to return to work while still injured. I often wondered how lawmakers who create these Workers' Compensation laws would feel if they were treated similarly.

Crushed Dreams: A Workers' Compensation Nightmare

I'm certain they wouldn't tolerate it. If a politician were injured like my husband, it would likely be headline news and widely covered by media. Yet, when regular hard-working people are severely injured on the job, their plight often goes unnoticed.

I contacted several newspapers and news stations to cover our story, but they were uninterested in a story involving Workers' Compensation. This lack of media attention seemed to avoid exposing the unfair treatment of injured workers by insurance companies and politicians. We learned that Workers' Compensation is supposed to pay 66% of one's wages, but due to a cap imposed by the Arkansas House of Representatives, higher-paid employees like my husband received significantly less. In fact, he only received 32% of his pay, which is 34% less than other injured employees.

During election years, I noticed politicians campaigning at schools, promising care and good futures for young people. Yet, these same laws discriminate against those who have advanced in their careers, paying them much less if injured. This contradiction hardly shows care for the future of young people or those supporting families.

True care would involve passing laws that ensure fair and equal pay for injured workers, protecting careers, providing timely and comprehensive medical treatment without delays or denials, and not imposing financial burdens on workers and their families. The focus should shift from insurance companies to the injured worker. By removing the cap and ensuring all injured workers receive a fair and equal 66% of their pay, no injured worker would be compensated less than another. This solution seems simple, but the promises made during campaigning are seldom kept.

I was still on crutches, trying to push my husband around in his wheelchair when he went to his doctor's appointments. We must have been a sight, the two of us, but even in the hardest times, we were making it together. Real love can get you through anything. When a couple takes those vows – for better or worse, in sickness and in health – you never truly know when life will throw you a curveball. We had enjoyed plenty of good times and had been quite fortunate. I guess we were now experiencing some of those 'for better or worse' times. We were leaning on each other for strength.

I became persistent with Tracy's Workers' Compensation case manager, constantly calling, texting, and emailing about getting him treatment. Finally, after a month of asking, they ordered an MRI for his knee at the end of November, a whole month after the injury. The MRI results showed torn ligaments in his knee, which remained red, hot to the touch, swollen, and very painful. After receiving these results, the doctor scheduled his knee surgery for the end of December, nearly two months after the injury.

As of November 28, 2018, Tracy still hadn't received any treatment for his back. He kept mentioning his back pain at every appointment, asking when it would be addressed. Despite his pleas, his Workers' Compensation case worker made no arrangements for his back treatment. Finally, I made an appointment with our family doctor. Tracy saw another doctor within the same practice. I explained Tracy's anxiety, nightmares, sleep disturbances, and back pain. The doctor diagnosed him with PTSD from the crushing incident and prescribed medication to help.

The doctor stressed the importance of getting Workers' Compensation to treat his back, but I knew that was easier said than done. Despite our repeated requests for his back to be examined, nothing had been done. It seemed like Workers' Compensation was hoping injured individuals would seek treatment elsewhere, thereby absolving them of payment responsibilities. This approach, categorizing external treatment as "unauthorized," was frustrating. Injured individuals need timely treatment, and Workers' Compensation companies should be held accountable for providing and paying for this essential care.

Chapter 14

In mid-November, we were getting ready for bed one night when our oldest son, who has heart problems and had been sick, came into our bedroom looking extremely pale. He said he wasn't feeling well, and suddenly he collapsed, having a seizure. I tried to get off the bed, yelling for Tracy to call 911. Tracy dialed 911 and put it on speakerphone. I informed the operator that our son had a bad heart and was experiencing a seizure.

By the time the ambulance arrived, the seizure had stopped, and he was sitting on the floor, still pale and shaking. The paramedics asked what had happened, and I explained his illness and heart condition. When I mentioned his new prescription cough syrup, a paramedic immediately asked to see it and pointed out that it shouldn't have been taken with his heart medication, likely causing the seizure. At the hospital, the doctor also confirmed that the two medications should not have been mixed and expressed surprise that the pharmacy hadn't caught the mistake.

The next day, I confronted the pharmacy, questioning why they hadn't noticed the dangerous combination when both prescriptions were filled there. The pharmacist admitted their oversight, which was alarming considering the potentially life-threatening consequences.

Our son had received the cough syrup from an urgent care clinic, where he informed them of his heart medication. It was concerning that the urgent care doctor also failed to recognize the harmful interaction. We always used the same pharmacy for all his prescriptions, assuming they would catch any interactions.

Fortunately, the seizure didn't have more severe consequences, but it was a stark reminder of the importance of careful medication management. Amidst these challenges, our daughter, who was scheduled for treatment for her Mastocytosis, faced another hurdle. When she arrived at the cancer center in early December, we discovered that our insurance had been canceled. This cancellation happened sometime after Tracy's injury, unbeknownst to us, affecting our youngest two adult children covered under the family plan.

As a result, our daughter couldn't undergo her scheduled 2-3 hour IV treatment. Instead, she had to switch to daily stomach injections for four weeks, costing $60 per weekly bottle. I administered these injections, which left her stomach bruised and sore by the end of the month. My heart ached for her. She would need a spinal tap as soon as she acquired new insurance. Additionally, more spots characteristic of Mastocytosis were appearing on her skin.

Throughout these ordeals, it felt like we were constantly battling one difficulty after another, as if some malevolent force was working overtime against us.

Chapter 15

Before my husband's injury, I always thought Workers' Compensation would take good care of you if you got hurt on the job. It's easy to have that belief if you've never had to use it. However, after my husband's experience with Workers' Compensation, my perspective completely changed. It seems that Workers' Compensation may work adequately for minor injuries, but in cases of multiple injuries, the situation becomes significantly more complex and challenging.

We joined a Workers' Compensation group to communicate with other injured workers and learned a lot from their experiences. Injuries like a broken arm, where recovery is around eight to twelve weeks, often result in straightforward Workers' Compensation processes. However, with multiple injuries, we heard numerous horror stories about the difficulties in dealing with Workers' Compensation. In our case, getting coverage for all of Tracy's injuries was an uphill battle. Despite clear evidence from the accident scene video and ER reports stating lower extremities and back injuries, there were hurdles in getting everything covered.

Insurance companies often exploit loopholes to avoid covering costly injuries. Tracy consistently mentioned all his injuries at every doctor's visit and to his home health nurse. I have text messages showing our repeated requests to the Workers' Compensation case worker for back injury treatment. These experiences have led me to believe that the laws in our state, and probably many others, need to change. One critical reform should be imposing substantial fines on insurance companies that deny documented injuries. If Workers' Compensation is the only recourse for injured workers, then these companies must provide care for each injury without forcing individuals to seek what they consider "unauthorized treatment." Injured people cannot wait months or years for treatment.

If insurance companies initially accepted and treated the injuries, there would be no need for seeking unauthorized treatments. As long as insurance companies are allowed to deny treatment to avoid payments, they will continue to do so. Since suing an employer is not an option under Workers' Compensation, lawmakers must ensure that injured employees receive all benefits that the employer's Workers' Compensation policy covers.

It's time for the House of Representatives in each state to become a voice for the INJURED WORKER. They need to stop allowing insurance companies to use these "tactics" or "loopholes" to evade paying for injuries. The current system is unfair and needs urgent reform.

Accompanying my daughter to her appointments, taking Tracy to his, and caring for my 80-year-old mother who was in congestive heart failure and starting to show signs of early dementia was overwhelming. I lived only half a mile from my mom, so I checked on her a couple of times daily, ensuring she took her morning and afternoon medications. Being the only person available to manage all this was incredibly challenging.

It was, to say the least, a rough period. Praying and talking to God were the only things that helped me get through each day. Our family was in dire need of many prayers – not just for healing and good health, but also for financial assistance. When it was time to turn on our furnace, we found out our central air and heat system was broken, and we didn't have the money to repair it. Then, floor joists in the kitchen and bathroom broke. The house was older, and the lack of a moisture barrier, combined with the previous owners running the dryer under the house, likely caused the joists to dry rot. It felt like everything was breaking left and right with no funds for repairs.

It seemed like our family just couldn't catch a break; we felt like we were drowning. We relied heavily on prayers during this time, drawing strength from Isaiah 40:29: "He gives power to the faint; and to them that have no might, he increases strength." We needed to put on the whole armor of God: that ye may be able to stand against the wiles of the devil. For we wrestle not against flesh and blood, but against principalities, against powers, against the rulers of the darkness of this world, against spiritual wickedness in high places. Wherefore take unto you the whole armor of God, that ye may be able to withstand in the evil day, and having done all, to stand.

Crushed Dreams: A Workers' Compensation Nightmare

In Jesus' name, I prayed fervently. We asked friends and family to pray for us and were added to our church's prayer list. The power of prayer and community support was what we leaned on in these trying times.

Chapter 16

In December, we were still waiting for Tracy to receive treatment for his back, but there was still no progress. The insurance companies' apparent strategy to make injured persons feel hopeless, by delaying or denying treatment, baffled us. How were they expected to recover? Tracy continued to visit his family doctor, pleading for help with his back pain. Unfortunately, she expressed her inability to assist due to Workers' Compensation constraints, saying her hands were tied by the system.

We questioned how Tracy was supposed to cope without proper treatment. It seemed that the House of Representatives expected injured individuals to suffer in silence, enduring excruciating pain without complaint. The reality of not receiving treatment simply because Workers' Compensation was responsible for payment was deeply frustrating.

Finally, at the end of December, Tracy underwent surgery on his knee, two months after the injury. The doctor repaired some ligaments but warned that a total knee replacement might be necessary in the future. The damage was more severe than the MRI had shown, likely exacerbated by the delay in treatment.

During this time, I was still on crutches when the office personnel from Tracy's employer called to inquire about his return to work. It had been only two months since his accident, and he was expected to be off for at least six months due to the surgery alone. I explained that Tracy had just undergone his second surgery and still hadn't received any treatment for his back. He was still confined to a wheelchair and undergoing home healthcare and physical therapy. The employer's expectation for his return to work under these circumstances seemed unrealistic.

To our dismay, she then informed me that the employer would be terminating the insurance coverage for me, the spouse. The children's coverage had already been cut off, and now they were discontinuing mine, only retaining Tracy's since he was still technically employed. This decision meant I could no longer attend my own medical appointments or continue physical therapy for my injured ankle.

Our financial situation was deteriorating rapidly. Tracy's Workers' Compensation check, reduced due to the CAP imposed by the House of Representatives, wasn't covering all our bills. We didn't qualify for food stamps or Medicaid, despite being just a couple of dollars over the eligibility limit. We were quickly falling behind on bills, depleting our savings, and even had to drain the account we had set up for our granddaughters. Our checking account was overdrawn, and we barely had money left for food or gas.

This situation led me to believe that every working person needs to start demanding better, fairer, and more equitable laws for injured workers from their state representatives. If we all use our voices to stand up for each other, we can make a significant impact. Imagine the effect if even just 100 people in each state called their representatives daily for a year to advocate for improved Workers' Compensation laws. Flooding their emails and leaving messages every day could prompt them to enact better protections for injured workers.

On Workers' Compensation, there are five classification levels that assess the severity of an injury, with class five representing the most severe cases. On January 3, 2019, at Tracy's doctor's appointment, he was classified as class five, indicating the most severe injury level. This classification remained unchanged at his January 10, 2019 appointment. Despite consistently reporting back pain, no arrangements were made for his back to be treated. On January 16, 2019, Tracy reported to the home health nurse and physical therapist that his back was not being treated, which they documented in their paperwork.

By February 12, 2019, Tracy was still in a wheelchair that was too small due to persistent swelling. We arrived 10 minutes early for his appointment, but after 30 minutes, Tracy hadn't been called back. I learned from the receptionist that the delay was because the Workers' Compensation nurse caseworker was running late and didn't want Tracy to be seen without her presence. I insisted that Tracy be seen as he was in discomfort and had arrived

Crushed Dreams: A Workers' Compensation Nightmare

on time for his appointment. Despite my insistence, we were made to wait.

An hour past the scheduled appointment time, the Workers' Compensation nurse finally arrived, and Tracy was immediately called back for his appointment. In the examination room, Tracy expressed his frustration to the nurse caseworker about the unnecessary delay and the discomfort caused by the inadequate wheelchair. He firmly stated that in the future, if he was on time for an appointment, he expected to be seen regardless of the caseworker's attendance.

Additionally, I addressed the issue of unpaid bills for the wheelchair rental, bedside commode, and shower bench. The caseworker assured us these would be taken care of, but the rental company continued to send threatening letters for three more months, warning of collections. Despite the caseworker's promises, it took Workers' Compensation four months to finally settle these bills. The stress of these unresolved issues, coupled with Tracy's ongoing pain and inadequate treatment, added significantly to our difficulties during this challenging period.

On February 13, 2019, the same supervisor who had previously suggested that Tracy's injury was due to hurrying sent him a text message that read, "you better hurry up and get well, this work is building up on you."

This message was received while my husband was still in a wheelchair, seeking medical care for his injuries. It's worth noting that Tracy was injured on the job by another employee who had been instructed to stop.

This particular supervisor had a history of delegating tasks but avoiding doing them personally. The employer often portrayed himself as a Christian, emphasizing words of faith. However, as the saying goes, "actions speak louder than words." While words may convey one's character, actions ultimately define it.

I had informed the receptionist back in December that Tracy was not ready to return to work, and there had been little improvement in his condition since then. It's perplexing how they expected him to expedite his return when he had waited two months for a knee operation that did not fully resolve the issue, and his back had received no treatment at all.

Returning to work was impossible if he remained injured and without proper treatment. At each appointment, Tracy received a work note indicating his condition: class five with severe limitations, incapable of Secretarial work, and no work recommended at this time. His hip, knee, and back continued to ail him, with no efforts from Workers' Compensation to address the back injury.

Upon returning from the doctor's appointment, Tracy was deeply frustrated. He expressed his intention to seek legal counsel as he had not received any treatment for his back, despite the accident occurring four months prior. The events of that day's appointment had left him feeling that such inaction was inexcusable, leading him to contact an attorney.

On March 7, 2019, during our appointment, the Workers' Compensation nurse informed us that she could no longer attend our appointments due to our decision to hire an attorney. Despite this development, Tracy's condition remained classified as class five with severe limitations.

In March, Tracy had the idea to request the accident report from OSHA to provide our attorney with additional information about the accident that occurred on October 26, 2018. Recognizing the potential value of this report for our attorney, I agreed, and Tracy proceeded to contact OSHA to request the accident report.

OSHA assured us that they would send the necessary information. Meanwhile, in March, our daughter, who was pregnant with our grandson, faced a health challenge. She had developed preeclampsia at just 32 weeks into her pregnancy. The medical team aimed to help her reach at least 36 weeks of pregnancy before delivery. We placed our daughter and our grandson, named Jacob, on the prayer list at our church, fervently praying for their well-being.

By the time she reached 35 weeks, the medical team began administering injections to strengthen Jacob's lungs. One week later, at exactly 36 weeks, she was sent to the hospital for induced labor, and Jacob was born safely and in good health. The doctor noted that there was an issue with his placenta, which should have been detected during the 20-week anatomy scan. Given the circumstances, he should have been delivered by c-section.

We celebrated the arrival of Jacob, a true blessing, and our daughter's family was now complete with a boy and a girl. It was a joyous moment for their beautiful little family.

Chapter 17

March and April passed by without any significant developments. However, on May 1, 2019, we received a letter from OSHA that stated they couldn't send a report because the accident had never been reported by Tracy's employer. Consequently, the accident couldn't be investigated properly, and the company would receive only a small fine.

In hindsight, we wondered if this was the reason why the supervisor had initially claimed that my husband had been in a hurry and that's what caused the accident. Looking back, numerous aspects of this accident appeared mishandled. The proper procedures following an accident were not followed.

Firstly, I should have been notified by the employer immediately, rather than another employee contacting me hours later after my husband was injured. Furthermore, the employer, who arrived at the scene, should have called me, and they should have promptly reported the accident to OSHA. Additionally, the employee responsible for the accident should have been immediately subjected to a drug and alcohol test.

Over the years, my husband had witnessed instances where employees at this company were caught drinking during their lunch breaks or even on the job. In such cases, they were sent home. Tracy's accident occurred shortly after lunch, which raises the question of whether the other employee involved may have been under the influence, affecting their judgment.

Why didn't the employer do the responsible and right thing by reporting the accident to OSHA within the required twenty-four hours? We now know that it was not reported, as confirmed by the letter from OSHA. We will never know if the other employee was subjected to a drug or alcohol test because the company refused to provide my husband with the accident report they are required to keep on file at their office.

What we do know is that my husband deserved to have this accident investigated by OSHA. His blood was drawn at the hospital and analyzed for drugs or alcohol at the request of Workers' Compensation, which showed no traces of either. If the injured party has to undergo a drug and alcohol test, the same rules should apply when a work-related accident involves more than one person, and the person who caused the injury should be subjected to the same standards.

The injured individual deserves to know if the other employee involved was under the influence, which seems reasonable and should be mandatory. If that employee was indeed under the influence, then the company should have been held liable. Unfortunately, nothing was done to protect my husband's rights, indicating a double standard.

Employers have a moral obligation to do the right thing, and promptly reporting an accident to OSHA for investigation is undoubtedly the right thing to do. Unfortunately, it appears that these laws are not consistently enforced.

I've spoken with many people on social media who have experienced injuries and faced similar problems. This seems to be a widespread issue. My husband never expected this to happen to him after being cautious for thirty years, but it only takes one unsafe employee to change your life.

How many more people have to suffer before we all acknowledge that the Workers' Compensation system needs a major overhaul, and injured workers should receive the protection they rightfully deserve?

On March 8, 2019, I informed our family doctor that Tracy was still not receiving any treatment for his back.

Then, on March 21, 2019, Tracy had another doctor's appointment, and once again, the Workers' Compensation work note indicated that he was at class five, which meant he was still unable to work. This was consistent with all the previous appointments.

After our appointment, as we were checking out, the Workers' Compensation nurse showed up and began talking to the doctor in the hallway. She was right behind us, so we could overhear their conversation. The nurse caseworker requested that the doctor change his note to indicate that she believed Tracy could return to work.

The doctor, however, disagreed and said, "I don't believe he can return to work; that's why I marked it as class five, indicating no work at this time." This response didn't sit well with the nurse caseworker, who lost her temper. She started yelling, stomping her foot, and even pointed in the doctor's face. It was like watching a toddler throw a tantrum. The doctor sternly told her to stop, reminding her that he had other patients and wouldn't tolerate such behavior.

We left the doctor's office with the doctor's note still indicating that Tracy was at class five, unable to work. However, a couple of weeks later, when we requested all of the medical records from this doctor to provide to our attorney, we discovered that the doctor had altered the paperwork from the March 21, 2019 appointment. Apparently, he made these changes after we had left the appointment, despite initially disagreeing with the nurse caseworker.

The note was changed from class five, indicating severe limitations, to class four, indicating moderate limitations, and the words "Desk work only" were added. This change occurred because the Workers' Compensation nurse caseworker had thrown a tantrum and demanded it. It raises questions about the legality of doctors changing paperwork to benefit Workers' Compensation when it doesn't reflect the patient's actual condition.

We still possess the original doctor's note, as well as the altered note that was placed in Tracy's medical chart to replace the original. The altered note was submitted to Workers' Compensation. The fact that such changes were made without any corresponding change in Tracy's health within minutes is concerning.

We've provided both notes to our attorney and shared copies with two House of Representatives members to highlight the dishonest and corrupt practices that occur. It's alarming to think about how often this might happen without workers having any proof.

I've reached out to several House of Representatives members through emails, calls, text messages, and social media messages, sharing my husband's story. While approximately half of the representatives have received information about my husband's accident and the mistreatment of injured workers, no concrete actions have been taken to address these issues.

It's time for the necessary changes to be made, and there are no excuses for inaction. The House of Representatives needs to take action and address these ongoing problems with the Workers' Compensation system. Many people have raised concerns, and it's imperative that their voices are heard and acted upon.

During this time, I found myself juggling multiple responsibilities. I was not only taking care of Tracy but also shuttling my mom to her cardiologist appointments and accompanying her for cataract surgeries, one eye at a time. Additionally, I supported my daughter during her spinal tap procedure and tried to be there for her doctor's appointments at the cancer center when possible. It seemed like I had appointments marked on the calendar at least 3-4 times a week, thanks to Tracy, my mom, and my daughter.

On April 23, 2019, when Tracy attended his doctor's appointment, the doctor expressed his frustration with working with Workers' Compensation insurance. He acknowledged that Tracy would eventually require knee and hip replacements due to his injury but felt there was nothing more he could do for him. What he could have done was stand up to Workers' Compensation and resist changing the doctor's note. Unfortunately, he yielded, and Workers' Compensation prevailed once again.

It's astonishing how this system works. Now, the doctor had labeled Tracy as Maximum Medical Improvement (MMI), even though Tracy wasn't fully recovered. He had just started using a walker, his back had received no treatment, and he still faced issues with his knee and hip. Despite this, the doctor dismissed him as a patient, and once you're classified as MMI, Workers' Compensation discontinues the benefits.

Tracy remained injured, hadn't received treatment for his back, and was now without a treating doctor. He was in no condition to return to work, and yet, his Workers' Compensation benefits were cut off.

On that very same day, April 23, 2019, Tracy's employer made the shocking decision to terminate his employment. Yes, they fired him. This left an injured employee, still not fully recovered, unable to work, and without a Workers' Compensation check. It's truly a remarkable system, and these representatives certainly know how to advocate for injured workers.

With Workers' Compensation cutting off his check and us having no income, we finally became eligible for Medicaid. Thanks to the assistance of one of our state's House of Representatives, we were able to secure Medicaid within just a couple of days. It was a relief to see a representative step in and help us with something.

Tracy reached out to his attorney to discuss the lack of treatment for his back injury. His attorney informed him that both Workers' Compensation and his employer had denied the back injury. She advised him to seek treatment if necessary, as she believed Workers' Compensation would have to cover it in the end. Attorneys provide advice based on their knowledge of the laws, and in this case, we followed her guidance.

However, it turned out that seeking treatment outside of approval was considered "unauthorized treatment" under the laws. So, despite the assurance that it would eventually be covered, we found out four years later that they didn't have to pay for anything because the judge deemed it unauthorized treatment. It seems much easier for the system to allow insurance companies to avoid accountability for delaying treatment and denying documented injuries. This extended legal process appears to work in their favor.

All of this makes you question the entire system. It certainly doesn't seem designed to benefit injured workers, especially since Tracy was labeled as Maximum Medical Improvement (MMI).

Chapter 18

On May 2, 2019, our family doctor, who has been a caring presence in our lives for the past twelve years, was finally able to order an MRI for Tracy's back. It had been a long wait, but a couple of weeks later, Tracy underwent the MRI, and the report revealed significant damage. His family doctor then referred Tracy to a neurologist, who, in my opinion, is the best, kindest, and most caring neurologist one could hope for. This neurologist displayed exceptional compassion, and finally, after six almost seven months of delayed and denied treatment, Tracy was about to receive medical care for his injured back.

It's baffling that an injured person, hurt on the job, had to endure nearly seven months of waiting to receive medical treatment for his back. Meanwhile, his attorney would be filing paperwork to dispute the denial of the back injury and to reinstate his Workers' Compensation check. Tracy's neurologist was located in Little Rock, over an hour and a half drive away. Financially, we were struggling because neither Tracy nor I could work at that time.

Although Workers' Compensation is supposed to reimburse all mileage for doctors' appointments, physical therapy, surgeries, etc., they refused due to their denial of treatment. To understand our rights, I purchased the Arkansas Workers' Compensation book used by attorneys and began researching the laws. According to the book on page twenty-nine, it clearly states that every injury to an employee arising out of and in the course of their employment should have all treatment covered. This includes any new injuries resulting from an incident. It's only logical that anyone severely hurt would seek treatment. No elected official would want to endure what my husband experienced, yet the laws make it incredibly challenging for injured workers to access the treatment they require.

During this challenging time, we received support from Tracy's wonderful aunt and uncle who offered financial assistance. I had also started selling small items to help make ends meet, but it wasn't enough. Unfortunately, I fell two months behind on our mortgage, and a third month was looming, along with the threat of foreclosure.

On a Friday, I turned to prayer, pleading with God to help us avoid losing our home and becoming homeless. We were about to fall three months behind on our mortgage, had no money for the electric bill, water bill, or phone bill. It was a frightening moment, and we had never felt so financially strained. I had to place my trust in the Lord and have faith that He would provide, as He had done many times before.

Over that Friday and Saturday, I prayed fervently, asking the Lord to hear my pleas. By Sunday night, after taking my mom to the store, we had about $100 left, which Tracy's aunt and uncle had given me. I spent $94.97 in the store, leaving us with just $5. I felt even more discouraged.

As I left the store with my mom, an elderly couple passed by. I was in my walking boot, having recently gotten off crutches, and I was carrying the few bags of groceries. The elderly man made a lighthearted comment, suggesting I put the bags in their car. I replied, "I can't; this is all I have, and my husband is out of work." His response stunned me, as he suggested Tracy should find a job. I quickly walked away, holding back tears.

To my surprise, the couple turned around and followed me back to my car. As we reached my car, the elderly man, who had worked for the railroad for over forty years, asked what kind of work Tracy did. I shared how Tracy had been hurt and had worked as a heavy equipment mechanic for thirty years. I didn't mention our financial struggles, only the extent of Tracy's injuries and my recent recovery from crutches.

The couple was incredibly kind and asked if we could all hold hands and pray together. I eagerly agreed, as we could use all the prayers we could get. In that parking lot, at our car's trunk, we held hands and prayed together. Afterward, they asked if they could add us to their church's prayer list, and I accepted. They also requested my phone number, and I willingly shared it.

Our daughter, who had been visiting, expressed concerns about giving out personal information. She joked that if she didn't hear from me, she'd assume we'd been murdered because she watched too much crime television. We assured her it was highly unlikely that this elderly couple singled me out at the store to harm us. We shared a quirky sense of humor in our family.

The couple drove an hour to our house, and once they arrived, I invited them in. We spent time together, prayed, and engaged in small talk. About twenty minutes into their visit, the wife suddenly said, "God sent us to help you," and mentioned that they wanted to provide financial assistance. I had prayed for God's help, and it seemed that my prayers were being answered.

They handed me a check, made out in my name, but I didn't look at the amount until after they left. When I finally saw it, I was overwhelmed with emotion and gratitude. I immediately thanked God for sending them our way. The check was enough to catch up on the mortgage, pay the electric, water, and phone bills, buy groceries for a few weeks, restock some essentials, and fill the gas tank for Tracy's upcoming medical appointments. It was a much-needed blessing.

Many might consider this a coincidence, but I firmly believe it was an answer to our prayers. I have no doubt that God heard our pleas and sent these kind-hearted individuals to help us. God places people where they are needed most, and we will forever be grateful to this couple. They requested that we not disclose their names but encouraged us to pay it forward if we ever had the means to help someone else in need.

I continue to sing at our church, and my husband and I attended their church a few weeks later. I sang for their congregation, and we enjoyed fellowship together. We even visited their home a few weeks after that. Our bond has remained strong, and we frequently exchange cards for holidays or just to provide updates on Tracy's progress. They always respond with warmth and support. We keep each other in our prayers.

We will never forget the generosity and kindness of this couple. They will always hold a special place in both our hearts. Thank you, Lord, for hearing and answering our prayers and for sending these wonderful people into our lives. This couple truly embodied the spirit of compassion and love, and their assistance made a significant difference in our lives during a challenging time.

Tracy's check was still cut off, and the bills were right back the very next month. It pained us greatly, but Tracy and I made a difficult decision. We decided to sell Tracy's service truck, which we had just paid off two weeks before his accident.

The truck was in good condition but had high mileage. Tracy had always taken excellent care of his service trucks, and they usually lasted a long time despite the high mileage. However, we knew the high mileage would affect the selling price, but we had no other choice. Tracy had a preference for FORD when choosing a service truck, and this one had a crane welder and many extras. Even though it was still running well, the mileage of 429,000 prevented us from getting the best price. We needed the money, so I sold it for what I knew was only half of its actual value, but it would help us get through this tough period.

It was heart-wrenching to part with the things my husband had worked so hard for, but we believed that God had blessed us with those possessions and was now providing a way for us to navigate these difficult times. Over the next couple of months, our attorney continued working to get Tracy's Workers' Compensation check reinstated. We had been through so much – first selling his service truck, then some of his tools, and even his jet skis. The financial strain was immense, but I was determined not to lose our home.

Watching the person you love struggle physically, emotionally, and mentally, while also drowning financially, is extremely difficult. We were living on faith, trusting that the Lord would see us through. During this time, we were immensely grateful for those who helped us financially. We didn't know how we would make it, but we kept our faith that the Lord would pull us through, and that's exactly what happened.

My elderly mom, Tracy's aunt and uncle, my sister, our children when they could, and two small love offerings from our home church provided the financial support we needed. Additionally, a kind elderly couple, complete strangers, also extended their help. These are what true Christians look like, and while it can be challenging to find genuine believers, they are out there. We are thankful for those who are true to their faith and reach out to help others in their time of need. It's during difficult times that you discover who your true friends and family are.

I reached out to several foundations and organizations, explaining Tracy's injuries and our situation. I asked for assistance with home repairs or building materials. Unfortunately, most of them could only help injured military personnel, and because Tracy's accident was not military-related, we did not qualify. While I deeply appreciate the programs and foundations that assist our injured military, I wished there were similar options for those injured in different types of accidents.

I contacted numerous foundations and organizations, but only one offered a small donation of $500. They recognized it was a modest amount and explained that their primary focus was helping injured military personnel. Nevertheless, we were grateful for their contribution. I also reached out to television shows and hosts, hoping to share our story, but received no response.

At this point, it felt like we were stuck with numerous home repairs and no means to address them. This was one of the lowest points in our lives. We had always been self-sufficient and able to overcome our challenges, but the scale of our problems was overwhelming. Without the Lord to talk to and our faith that we would overcome these difficulties, it's easy for a person to sink into a dark place.

I decided to shift my focus and see if I could do something about the issues we faced with Workers' Compensation in our state. Maybe Tracy's accident could raise awareness. I resumed emailing the House of Representatives in our state. However, it became evident that most of the representatives had limited knowledge of Workers' Compensation, often responding with, "I don't know."

Living with an injury and navigating Workers' Compensation had taught me a lot. Life had become my best teacher. Researching and reading the Workers' Compensation book helped me understand what should have been done compared to what actually happened. Most representatives I talked to lacked concrete answers. When I shared my husband's treatment experiences, their responses were often, "that can't be right," or "that doesn't seem fair." It certainly didn't seem fair, but unfortunately, that was the reality.

One representative condescendingly stated, "I strongly feel there is nothing wrong with the Workers' Compensation laws, and they don't need any changes, but thanks for calling." Another suggested getting an attorney if I believed the laws were unfair. However, attorneys can only work within the framework of existing laws. The real issue was holding representatives accountable and ensuring that the state enforced laws to protect workers.

It baffled me how these legislators voted on matters that they themselves would never use, assuming it was beneficial for hardworking people who actually needed it. I continued to call and email representatives in my spare time. Two of them sat down with me and genuinely listened. I had printed out proof to support my statements, allowing them to see the evidence as I spoke. This approach seemed to resonate with them, and they agreed to try drafting a bill on a few issues I had raised. The legislative session was set to resume in 2023, and I hoped that real change might be on the horizon.

Chapter 19

In July 2018, Tracy came across a small car in Texarkana while he was working. The car needed a new transmission, so he purchased it and then found a used transmission with only 35,000 miles for $500. With the cost of the car and the transmission, we had invested $1,100 in it, which was a great deal for a car. Our SUV was accumulating high mileage, and we thought the small car could serve as a spare and save us on gas. It was an excellent little car with only 117,899 miles when we acquired it.

After Tracy's injury, I parked my SUV and started using the small car full-time due to its better fuel efficiency. However, on August 2, 2019, I had gone to town with my daughter Ashley and her baby Jacob (only 2 and a half months old) and Kimber (2 years old). On our way back home, about halfway there, the car in front of me came to a stop, waiting for a semi-truck to pass so it could turn into a driveway. I stopped behind that car.

Crushed Dreams: A Workers' Compensation Nightmare

As I glanced in my rear-view mirror, I saw an SUV approaching at full speed. I yelled to Ashley that we were going to get hit just as the SUV slammed into us without braking, sending our car spinning into the ditch. Baby Jacob started crying intensely, while Kimber seemed to be okay.

I quickly opened the door, got Jacob out of his car seat, and noticed that he was still crying. I was concerned that he might be hurt, given his crying. A passing car stopped, and the occupants mentioned they had called an ambulance. I handed Jacob to his mother, hoping she could comfort him. The driver and his friend from the SUV approached us, asking if the baby was okay. I replied that I wasn't sure and asked the driver if he had been on his phone since he hadn't attempted to brake.

The driver, with an ace bandage on his wrist, held up his wrist and mentioned that it was injured. I told him that a hurt wrist wouldn't prevent him from applying the brakes and that he should have seen me stopped. I suspected he had been on his phone, but sometimes young people lack common sense.

I warned him that he should hope my grandson wasn't hurt because of his lack of attention. When the police arrived, I informed them that the driver hadn't tried to stop and that I believed he had been on his phone. However, the officer said he couldn't check the driver's phone, as the driver had denied using it.

The ambulance arrived and examined Jacob, who had calmed down and stopped crying. Thankfully, he wasn't injured. The other driver received a ticket, and the police officer provided me with the other driver's insurance information, stating that he had full coverage.

Initially, when I contacted the other driver's insurance company, they assured me that everything would be taken care of. However, a couple of days later, our insurance company contacted me and explained that the vehicle's owner (the driver's dad) had signed a paper excluding his son from driving the vehicle. This action canceled out the full coverage, and the insurance wouldn't pay the claim if the son was driving and caused an accident.

Luckily, we had uninsured motorist coverage on our insurance policy, so it would cover the claim, and our insurance would bill both the dad and the driver for the amount they paid out on the claim. They would now be considered uninsured motorists.

Unfortunately, we were left without a small car to drive, so we had to search for another one for our doctor's appointments. Eventually, we found another car with the funds provided by our insurance payout.

The rest of 2019 was dedicated to seeing doctors for Tracy's knee, hip, and back issues, including visits to a neurologist and pain management specialists. In August, our daughter and son-in-law welcomed a healthy baby boy, marking our fourth grandchild. Despite the challenges we were facing, the joy of welcoming a new family member brought much-needed happiness. Children are always a beautiful blessing to a family, and we cherished the time spent with our handsome grandsons.

Tracy experienced troubling symptoms in his left leg, including numbness, a burning sensation, temperature fluctuations, and changes in appearance, sometimes turning blue and causing severe pain. He sought treatment from an orthopedic doctor in Little Rock on August 5, 2019, followed by appointments on August 8 and August 16. Another MRI on his knee was performed on August 21, 2019, in Little Rock. On August 30, 2019, he received the results from the MRI, revealing that he needed a total knee replacement.

Thanks to the attorney's efforts, Tracy underwent pre-testing for the knee replacement on September 4, 2019. He also continued to see a neurologist in Little Rock. However, on September 17, 2019, a setback occurred as Tracy was unable to proceed with the total knee replacement due to the discovery that he had developed diabetes, with an A1C level of 11.5. Tracy had never been diabetic before, but his inactivity in a wheelchair and being bedridden, coupled with weight gain resulting from his accident, contributed to this development.

To prepare for surgery, Tracy needed to bring his A1C levels under control. I immediately began researching natural ways to lower A1C levels. Tracy initiated a diet and started taking metformin, but I also explored additional natural remedies, including cinnamon pills and chia seeds. However, it's important to note that these methods worked for him but may not be suitable for everyone. Always consult with a healthcare provider before attempting any health-related treatments.

Tracy began taking two cinnamon pills daily, one with his morning medication and two with his evening medication. Additionally, he incorporated chia seeds into his diet, following the instructions on the package. Through these efforts and significant weight loss, he managed to lower his A1C level to 6.5 by the end of December. This achievement allowed him to receive approval for his total knee replacement. However, Workers' Compensation required an independent doctor's opinion before granting approval for the procedure.

Chapter 20

In November, I had finally healed enough to return to work, enabling me to endure an 8-hour shift. I chose to work at a factory as this income would be vital during the period when Tracy would undergo his total knee replacement. Initially, it was challenging to stand on concrete for the entire shift, and by the end, my ankle was so swollen that removing my boot became a struggle. The last couple of hours standing were particularly miserable, but I persevered out of necessity; we needed the money.

In December, our youngest daughter got engaged, and we were thrilled to welcome another son-in-law, Colby, into our family. Witnessing our fourth child find the love of her life was an exciting and joyous occasion for us. Despite our happiness for them, our home continued to face issues, and there was no extra money for repairs. Our kitchen, in particular, was in a dire state, with four broken floor joists. I felt embarrassed by the condition of our house, but we had to make do. I continued to reach out to various resources in our state via email, but unfortunately, no one was willing to provide assistance.

Fortunately, our attorney succeeded in reinstating Tracy's Workers' Compensation check. While he didn't receive the back pay he was owed, having the check back was a relief. With the first check, I purchased a larger wheelchair for Tracy to use when needed. Although he could walk, long distances were painful, and he often required a wheelchair for mobility, especially when we went out. Most of the time, he preferred to stay home.

We had an appointment to see an independent doctor for a second opinion requested by Workers' Compensation. During the appointment, we noticed a substantial and, frankly, an outrageous amount attached to the paperwork as payment for the second opinion. This raised questions, especially considering that Tracy was owed over two months' worth of back pay, which Workers' Compensation had not paid. The doctor conducted an examination and reviewed Tracy's MRI. Fortunately, the exorbitant payment did not influence the doctor's medical opinion, and he concurred with the first doctor that Tracy unequivocally needed a total knee replacement.

In January, we attended Tracy's pre-surgery testing, and this time, all the tests returned with positive results. His A1C level was 6.2, signaling that the surgery was a go. In February 2020, he would undergo his total knee replacement. On the day of surgery, we prayed for a successful procedure, and Tracy went in for the operation.

After the surgery, Tracy experienced an immense amount of pain. His IV fell out, and it took six attempts to reinsert it.

Eventually, another nurse with an ultrasound located the vein and successfully reinserted the IV. Tracy has a history of post-surgery nausea due to anesthesia, and this time was no exception; he vomited.

In the hours following surgery, the pain intensified, particularly in the area where the torque was placed. The first two weeks were excruciating for Tracy, and he found it impossible to drive. Consequently, I had to resign from my job to ensure that I could transport Tracy to his numerous medical appointments. We were shuttling back and forth to Little Rock for visits with the orthopedic doctor three times a week, physical therapy sessions, consultations with the neurologist, pain management appointments for his back, back ablation, hip injections, lumbar injections, and two nerve studies on his upper thigh area, which had been severely injured.

I was also responsible for taking my mom to her cardiologist and family doctor appointments more frequently. It was during this time that Tracy received a diagnosis from his neurologist and pain management doctors: Complex Regional Pain Syndrome (CRPS), a debilitating nerve disease known for its extreme pain. CRPS can develop following a high-impact injury or after being crushed. It is infamously referred to as the "suicide disease" due to its excruciating nature.

CRPS typically affects the limbs and entails severe, disproportionate pain compared to the initial injury. On the McGill Pain Scale, it ranks at 45/50, surpassing the pain associated with childbirth or wartime limb amputation without anesthesia. Some other symptoms of CRPS include:

- allodynia: hypersensitivity to light touch
- hyperalgesia: extreme hypersensitivity to pain
- changes in hair and nail growth
- skin color changes
- skin texture changes
- temperature changes
- changes to sweating patterns
- stiffness in joints
- temporary paralysis
- delayed wound healing
- hypersensitivity to sounds and light
- irritability
- edema
- depression
- insomnia
- fatigue
- dystonia: involuntary muscle spasms causing a fixed contracture of a single extremity or multiple extremities
- myoclonus/tremors: the quick random jerking movements
- muscle atrophy

- osteopenia/osteoporosis: bone density loss due to reduced blood flow

- gastrointestinal problems

- failure to thrive

- weight gain/loss

Some doctors don't fully understand CRPS.

Despite Tracy's ongoing medical care, which included pain management, neurology, physical therapy, and orthopedics, his knee did not improve following the total knee replacement. It remained unstable, painful, and painful to walk on. During every orthopedic visit, Tracy expressed that the knee felt loose and something was amiss. Nevertheless, the doctor repeatedly insisted that the surgery had been performed correctly, even though his notes reflected Tracy's complaints of knee instability, pain, and correct surgery.

The repetition of the phrase "surgery was done correctly" left us questioning whether the doctor was attempting to convince us or himself. Finding dedicated and compassionate doctors has become a challenge in today's healthcare landscape, and we yearn for the kind of physicians who genuinely care for and support their patients. Our lives became consumed by constant medical appointments.

Chapter 21

My mom's dementia was worsening. I would visit her, but after I left, she would often leave her house and wander onto the road. This was concerning because our home was situated on a busy main road with heavy traffic. On one occasion, the police brought her to our house because she was walking in the middle of the road. My mother-in-law and step-father-in-law happened to pass by and informed the police about our address. They emphasized the need to keep her off the road. However, explaining this to a person with dementia proved challenging.

My mom had always been fiercely independent and cherished being in her own home. I tried to reason with her, emphasizing the danger of being on the road at her age and the potential harm to drivers if she were to fall in front of a car. While our talk would have a temporary effect, she would eventually return to walking on the road. She insisted that being on the road was not against the law, and neither the police nor I could dictate her actions.

We were fortunate to live in a small town where my mom resided across from the post office. The post office staff would alert us if she left her house. My schedule remained consistently busy, with only a day or two each month, along with weekends, where we weren't attending various medical appointments, including doctors' visits, physical therapy, and pain management sessions. When I wasn't accompanying Tracy to his appointments, I was shuttling my mom back and forth to her cardiologist, follow-up appointments for her cataract surgeries, and her eyeglasses appointments. Her dementia was progressively worsening, leading to more frequent visits to her cardiologist and family doctor.

I was also accompanying my daughter to her appointments at the cancer center for her Mastocytosis. Some people would question why I didn't return to work. I had worked for about four months after healing from my injury, but it became nearly impossible to find someone who could drive to all these appointments. Many people couldn't afford to miss work, and everyone had their own busy schedules. Unless you're experiencing it firsthand, it's challenging to comprehend the complexity of our situation.

The remainder of 2020 was consumed by accompanying Tracy to appointments with the neurologist, orthopedic doctor, and enduring months of continuous physical therapy. We continued with visits to the pain management clinic. During evenings, I persisted in contacting members of the House of Representatives by sending emails detailing my husband's story. On some days, I resorted to making phone calls. This effort allowed me to connect with several House of Representatives whom I hadn't spoken to previously.

One representative made a striking observation, stating that Workers' Compensation is not akin to winning the lottery. This resonated with me because Workers' Compensation did not alleviate our financial struggles; instead, it imposed financial burdens. The cap that limits compensation for high-paid employees is far from resembling a lottery. Workers' Compensation often evades reimbursing for mileage, delays and denies treatments, and authorizes only a fraction of necessary medical procedures. It's a system that feels like kicking an employee when they are already down.

While I never anticipated Workers' Compensation to be a lottery, I, like many injured workers, expected it to fulfill the benefits outlined in the policies or those legislated by the House of Representatives. These benefits include reimbursing all mileage related to employee injuries, covering all medications, doctor's appointments, surgeries, medical bills, and required medical devices. Furthermore, it should provide comprehensive coverage for physical therapy following job-related injuries and ensure that medical equipment fits the injured person, even if they have swollen body parts, until they no longer require such equipment. Workers should not have their income severed when they still require treatment and cannot return to work.

Insurance companies sell these policies, but they have found ways to avoid honoring them. Furthermore, legislators often fail to ensure that these policies are enforced. While we have a Workers' Compensation commission, when I reported that paperwork was being altered, I was merely told that the caseworker must have had a valid reason. In essence, they prioritize getting injured workers back to work as quickly as possible, irrespective of their actual condition. They've even pressured doctors to change their recommendations.

In these scenarios, the injured worker is invariably considered wrong, while the employer and insurance company are deemed right. It's imperative that there are resources in place to protect injured workers in such situations. When these cases reach Workers' Compensation judges, any unjust actions should be rectified. So, to the representative who declared that Workers' Compensation is not a lottery, I would agree wholeheartedly. It is far from resembling a lottery in any way.

It's worth noting that in other scenarios, such as car accidents or slip-and-fall incidents, individuals can sue for pain and suffering. However, there are no laws under Workers' Compensation to safeguard injured workers from deliberate actions by fellow employees. This highlights the undervaluation of an employee's life and their pain and suffering. I have witnessed my husband's daily suffering since this accident, and while no amount of money can restore his health, it could alleviate the financial burden imposed by the deliberate actions of another employee. That employee should have faced legal consequences for their actions.

Over time, I have received numerous comments on social media from injured workers who have faced similar challenges. I reiterate to the state House of Representatives: no injured individual should wait for 1, 2, 3, or 4 years, or more, to receive treatment when injured. If such a delay is deemed appropriate, I recommend that those voting on the matter experience it themselves the next time they fall ill or sustain an injury. When insurance companies deny treatment, it leads to injured individuals seeking "unauthorized treatment." I am confident that those voting on these issues would not tolerate such delays if they were in the injured person's shoes.

When insurance companies exploit loopholes to evade costs or legal obligations, injured workers are left in an unjust predicament. Our congressman for this district connected me with someone at the Workers' Compensation commission, who, unfortunately, staunchly supported the employer and insurance company. It was disheartening but unsurprising, given the biases at play. This individual seemed to assume that if the employer or insurance company asserted something, it must be true, while dismissing the employee's claims as false. This prevailing attitude is a matter that warrants serious reconsideration.

Because everything I conveyed to him, I must be mistaken. This was his stance: consistently defending the employer and insurance company, asserting that they are in the right, and that employees mustn't make it challenging for the employer or unfair to the insurance companies. Yes, he actually told me that they can't make it hard on the employers or insurance companies. Strangely, they don't seem to mind making it unfair or difficult for the injured worker.

I managed to find this individual's salary online; he worked at the Arkansas Workers' Compensation Commission and was making $95,000 a year. He was earning a substantial salary to support the employer and insurance company. I wish they worked just as diligently to ensure fairness for the injured worker. Talking to the worker at the commission turned out to be a futile endeavor.

If you visit the Arkansas State Workers' Compensation Commission website, it states: "The Arkansas Workers' Compensation Commission (AWCC) and the laws it administers were created effective December 5, 1940. Workers' Compensation insurance is directed towards the moral, social, and economic benefits of protecting employers, employees, and their dependents from financial burdens imposed by job-related injury and disease."

Based on my husband's experience with his injury, I find the statement about protecting employees and their dependents from financial burdens caused by job-related injuries to be questionable. However, the part about protecting employers appears to be a very honest and accurate statement. When the Arkansas House of Representatives imposed a cap on pay, severely injured high-paid employees, like my husband, received only 32% instead of the intended 66%. This amounted to a 34% reduction in compensation simply because they worked hard and advanced in their careers. Such unfair caps undeniably lead to financial burdens when they result in certain types of injured employees receiving less.

I propose that we should pay half of the representatives 66% of their pay for two years, and then cut the pay of the other half to 32% for two years. I'm certain none of them would remain content and would be very dissatisfied. Why is it that individuals who work diligently within a single profession, advance in their careers, and invest in education, always seem to come up short? We find ourselves in this predicament because we allow elected representatives to treat us this way.

If an injured employee is already subjected to receiving reduced compensation, and the insurance company is allowed to deny treatment and evade reimbursement for mileage to and from doctor's appointments, not paying for surgeries resulting from the work-related imposed injury, then how is the commission fulfilling its commitment to protect the injured employee from the financial burden, as stated on their website?

Another bill that Representatives passed stipulates that the pay remains the same as the year of the injury. Therefore, severely injured workers who are on Workers' Compensation for several years never receive a cost-of-living raise. Even people on Social Security receive such raises. For instance, if you were injured in the year 2000 and cannot return to work, you are stuck receiving what Workers' Compensation paid in 2000—no raise, regardless of the rising cost of living. This remains your pay, no matter the circumstances.

During the COVID pandemic, people who were out of work received an additional $600.00 in unemployment benefits because it was considered a financial hardship for them. People injured on the job face financial hardships and are also injured, yet legislators have decided that high-paid employees should not receive an extra $600 or the same 66% as other injured workers. Nor will they ever receive more than what their pay was in the year they were injured. Are these the same legislators who were outraged over COVID? Where is the outrage for injured workers?

Crushed Dreams: A Workers' Compensation Nightmare

When will they receive an extra $600 on top of their pay because they are facing financial hardships? Those same legislators do not apply the same logic here. I had another House of Representatives member tell me that injured workers should take more responsibility and ensure they have Aflac.

It is the employer's responsibility to maintain a Workers' Compensation policy that covers injuries sustained by their employees. Blaming the employee for not having Aflac is misplaced. Most hardworking individuals can't afford to take out extra insurance due to the high cost of living that American families are facing. Families are already struggling, and it's unreasonable for this representative to suggest that employees should provide extra insurance instead of holding Workers' Compensation insurance accountable for the policies they sell.

Many hardworking Americans are tired of seeing those who work the hardest being treated unfairly. Some politicians are allowed to enrich themselves while in office in ways that ordinary people would never get away with, potentially facing life imprisonment. Hardworking people are frustrated with how their hard-earned money is heavily taxed, with the funds seemingly going everywhere except to support hardworking individuals.

So, once again, this representative wants to place the blame on the injured person by suggesting they should simply take out Aflac. However, if I understand correctly, having Aflac may include an offset provision. In that case, Aflac wouldn't provide additional coverage to the employee; instead, it would help Workers' Compensation insurance companies pay even less. It's likely why this representative thinks Aflac would be beneficial, as anything that helps Workers' Compensation insurance pay less is something they support.

Instead of blaming injured workers, representatives should hold themselves accountable. The blame lies with representatives who vote to shortchange injured workers, using the excuse that they can't make it hard on employers or insurance companies. Passing better laws to ensure all workers receive fair and equal pay, preventing some from being paid less, and prohibiting insurance companies from using loopholes to deny or delay treatment for injured workers is the way forward.

I asked one representative a question on their Facebook page, but they didn't answer it; instead, they blocked me. This type of response is immature and avoids addressing valid concerns. Another representative called me after I waited six weeks for a response to my question about Workers' Compensation on his page. When I posted again and mentioned leaving a phone message, he became angry and yelled at me. I wasn't yelling during our conversation, and I had patiently waited six weeks before reaching out again. I simply wanted a response to my question, which seemed reasonable.

Some representatives seem to think that Workers' Compensation is not an urgent matter. However, it may not be urgent to them, but for those who suffer every day due to work-related injuries, it's a pressing concern. Many people have become homeless, struggled to pay their bills, contemplated suicide, and developed opioid addictions after being injured at work. These are real problems that should concern every state representative.

Crushed Dreams: A Workers' Compensation Nightmare

I have heard from many people in Arkansas and other states across the United States, and they all share a common desire: better laws for Workers' Compensation that ensure they receive all the benefits they are entitled to after being injured on the job. I have continually provided information to the two representatives who sat down with me, presenting each problem we faced to help them understand the challenges injured workers encounter.

I have reached out to them repeatedly, asking if something will be done to address these issues. One representative mentioned that he was working on a bill, drafting it for introduction in the 2023 session. Others face similar problems, making Workers' Compensation reform necessary.

One of the representatives I spoke with was a business owner who expressed shock at how injured workers are treated. He stated that this is not how he would want his employees to be treated if they were ever injured. He now has the opportunity to effect change as a state senator. By working together with other representatives, they can draft and pass new bills to correct the existing problems. They have the power to improve the lives of injured workers in Arkansas.

Other representatives in different states also have the power to help their constituents. Many representatives in Arkansas have now been made aware of these issues through my emails. The question now is, what will be done about it? What actions will representatives take to genuinely improve the situation?

As I've mentioned before, gaining a true understanding of something often requires experiencing it firsthand. The representative stated that he didn't understand why there was a CAP because he has always had to declare an employee's wage, and the employee's wage is the basis for determining Workers' Compensation premiums. While I haven't personally purchased Workers' Compensation insurance, I'm relaying what the representative explained to me. My understanding is that Workers' Compensation insurance premiums are calculated based on the employee's wage. Therefore, if an employer is paying more for a high-paid employee, it seems counterintuitive for that higher-paid employee to receive less compensation when they are injured.

The representative also mentioned that if the CAP were to be removed, insurance companies might argue that they would have to raise insurance premiums. However, since employers are already paying premiums based on their employees' wages, which should cover all employees being paid the full 66%, there may not be a need to increase premiums. It's possible that insurance companies would use this argument to discourage the removal of the CAP, as they often seek to deter actions that may reduce their profits.

I shared with another representative a book that attorneys use, containing all the relevant laws. I believe every representative should have access to such a resource because, before they vote on legislation, they should understand the specific language of the law and how it impacts injured workers. Additionally, they should actively listen to the real stories of injured workers to gain insight into their experiences.

I also propose the introduction of a new section of laws specifically addressing situations where an employee is intention-

Crushed Dreams: A Workers' Compensation Nightmare

ally harmed by another employee while on the job. This would provide additional protections and remedies for such cases.

Chapter 22

The Workers' Compensation commission holds an annual conference, and in 2019, their keynote speaker was an individual who had been injured in the military. Let me start by emphasizing my deep respect for our military personnel, as my father was a WWII veteran, and I hold immense appreciation for their service. I extend my thanks to all the men and women who have served our country; their dedication is truly valued. I want to make it clear that my comments are in no way intended to disrespect any military personnel.

The reason I bring up this matter is that military personnel do not typically use Workers' Compensation, and this particular individual did not reside in Arkansas. Therefore, it raises questions about how someone not familiar with Arkansas Workers' Compensation could effectively speak about the system at an Arkansas Workers' Compensation conference. While the military speaker may understand the experience of being injured and receiving care in the military context, they may not have the necessary insights

Crushed Dreams: A Workers' Compensation Nightmare

into the Arkansas Workers' Compensation system, which operates differently.

I would have liked to attend the conference and share my perspective, but the ticket prices were prohibitively high for us. It's important to consider the perspective of those who have actually navigated the Workers' Compensation system in Arkansas, as they can provide valuable insights based on their experiences.

Through my social media postings, I received a message from a fellow Arkansan named Scott Pitts, who suffered a severe work-related injury. He has given me permission to use his real name and share his story. Scott's life and his family's lives were forever changed by his workplace accident, and my heart goes out to him and his family.

According to Scott, the accident occurred on May 7, 2007, when he fell four stories, approximately forty-three feet, onto a concrete slab. He explained that he was working on a secured floor surrounded by cables. Unfortunately, another employee had removed the covering to an elevator shaft that was supposed to be in place. Scott had not noticed the absence of the covering, as it had always been there, making it a non-issue in his work routine. Tragically, this change resulted in the accident, as there was nothing to block the hole left by the removed covering.

Scott's injuries were extensive. He had to be airlifted to Little Rock, where he received five units of blood and remained in a coma for twenty-two days. He spent months in the ICU, during which time he saw fifteen different specialists. His injuries included broken arms and femurs, a crushed foot, a broken jaw, multiple broken teeth, fractured ribs (one of which collapsed his left lung), a lacerated liver, a punctured spleen, and an aorta rupture in the femoral corroded junction. Scott also suffered a 4-inch left leg discrepancy due to a severe femur splinter fracture. He underwent a total of 18 major surgeries.

Despite these severe injuries, some aspects of Scott's treatment were denied by Workers' Compensation, including the repair of his damaged teeth. He also did not receive reimbursement for some of his mileage expenses related to medical appointments. Like many others who have experienced work-related accidents, Scott faced significant financial burdens.

Scott recounted how his Workers' Compensation case nurse sometimes directed his doctor to limit his pain medication or not refill his much-needed pain medications. He was not provided with a pain management doctor, which resulted in him enduring constant pain. Scott's experiences resonated with me, as my husband also lives with constant pain due to his CRPS.

Scott mentioned that he had an appointment set up by Workers' Compensation, but when he arrived, his Workers' Compensation nurse case worker was already in the exam room with the doctor, which is not typically allowed. Scott's wife wheeled him back to the exam room, where the doctor and the Workers' Compensation caseworker nurse were waiting. The doctor's initial comment to Scott was unexpected and hurtful. He asked Scott if he knew what his biggest problem was, to which Scott replied that he did not, urging the doctor to share his perspective. The doctor's response was disheartening; he said, "that you survived." Scott recalled how those words deeply affected him, as they made him feel diminished and invalidated. I want to emphasize that individuals injured at work should not be condescended to or belittled by case workers or doctors.

Furthermore, Scott shared that another doctor had told him he would be better off dead, as it would spare him from enduring so much pain. It's incredibly challenging to face each day in excruciating pain, particularly when access to pain medication is limited or denied altogether. Scott mentioned that the doctor prescribed him either one Hydrocodone 10mg per day or two Hydrocodone 5mg per day, despite the extensive injuries he had suffered and the pain he endured.

It's crucial to note that the Workers' Compensation system typically does not provide compensation for pain and suffering when an individual is injured in a work-related accident. This means that those who experience such injuries may not receive adequate support for the immense physical and emotional challenges they face.

After a few years, his case was closed. During his Workers' Compensation journey, he encountered some of the same problems and challenges. Certain body parts were denied coverage, and he did not receive reimbursement for some of his mileage expenses. It was an incredibly trying period for him.

Another employee had removed something that should not have been touched, and as a result of this colleague's actions, Scott's health would never be the same. Despite the immense pain and suffering he endured, no compensation was provided. Scott found himself unable to work, and his life was forever altered.

While no amount of money can restore his health, individuals like Scott, my husband, and others who have suffered severe injuries due to someone else's actions should receive compensation for the life-altering effects of these injuries. The lifelong financial burdens, mental and emotional scars, and physical trauma resulting from such traumatic workplace injuries should not go uncompensated.

We are not alone in facing these challenges. Many injured workers, not just in our state but across the nation, confront similar issues. Individuals who endure multiple injuries suffer not only emotionally, mentally, and physically but also financially. Their lives are forever changed, and they often struggle to cope, with some even contemplating ending their lives, believing it might be better not to be here. It is crucial that no one is left to feel this way.

If you are experiencing suicidal thoughts, please always reach out to your doctor. You are important, and your loved ones need and want you to be here. I want to express my gratitude to Scott for allowing me to share his story with our readers, helping them understand the immense challenges he and his family have faced.

In the words of one of the representatives who said, "Workers' Compensation is not the lottery," you are correct. Workers' Compensation isn't the "lottery," nor should it be.

It certainly shouldn't cause those who are severely hurt by another employee or because of the actions of another employee, them or their families, to bear the financial consequences of another person's actions.

Crushed Dreams: A Workers' Compensation Nightmare

Not a single representative would want this to happen to them, and they wouldn't want one of their loved ones to go through this either. They shouldn't want or pass laws that would allow hardworking people in their state to experience such hardships. If a representative got hurt at the Capitol, all the media and newspapers would pick up the story. It would be front-page news. If their lives mean something, shouldn't the lives of all the hardworking people who voted for them also mean something?

My husband and I went to see his attorney, and she called the owner of the law firm to sit in on the meeting. The attorney acknowledges that the laws are unfair to injured workers, but claims their hands are tied. They are attorneys, so if they know it's "unfair," why don't they all band together to change it? I don't think they would do that. If the laws were fair, injured workers wouldn't need an attorney's assistance, so do they truly want the laws to change? Honestly, not much changed with the help of having an attorney.

I told the owner of the law firm that I was working with two legislators to try to change the unfair practices and discriminatory laws under Workers' Compensation. The owner of the law firm responded with a chuckle and a wink, saying, "good luck with that." He also mentioned that he could appreciate what I was trying to do, but seriously, one person can't make a difference, and nothing will change with Workers' Compensation until someone who is considered "important" gets hurt.

I sat there devastated as my heart sank, looking at him with a blank stare, tears rolling down my face. I was so angry inside, feeling like he just belittled regular working-class people. Do hardworking people not matter? Maybe one person can't make a difference, but at least I was trying. I tried to look away so they couldn't see my tears, but they did see, and the fact that it didn't affect them was disturbing. His attorney and the owner just looked at me.

I'm sure they are so used to telling injured people that the laws are just not written to protect injured workers that they have become numb to the feelings of their clients. Maybe one person can't make a difference, but if enough of us band together and stand up for injured workers, saying what they do is not right, maybe, just maybe, a whole lot of people together could make a difference.

One person can make a difference if they are an influential person, like a celebrity. When a celebrity gets hurt, you hear about it for days, it's all over social media, in the news, in newspapers. But ordinary hardworking, tax-paying workers, we are nothing, and nobody cares. Each and every one of the hardworking men and women who get up every day and go to work, no matter what kind of job you have, YOU MATTER! If you are working at a job, making an honest living to support your family, YOU MATTER, YOUR LIFE MATTERS! We are ALL IMPORTANT, even if they tell us we don't.

Who is this attorney to say that people like us aren't what "society deems important"? Maybe my hardworking mechanic husband isn't what this owner of this law firm thinks is important. But make no mistake; he was and is important to me as his wife. He is important to his children, to his grandchildren, to his parents, to his brothers and sisters, and to all who know and love him.

Crushed Dreams: A Workers' Compensation Nightmare

I certainly think my husband is important. I certainly think each of you are important.

Who is "What society deems important"? Only celebrities, doctors, attorneys, politicians, and rich people? WE THE PEOPLE who get up every day and work hard – if we are so unimportant to society, then quit robbing our paychecks. Stop taxing us to death. I'm so tired of hearing that we are so unimportant. When politicians are trying to get our vote, then we are important. After elected, they forget all about "we the people." Once elected, as little as possible is done to help the very people who elected them, and then they try to tell us how much they "care" for us and that they know what is best!

If they truly knew what was best, they would pass laws that protect us, not harm us. They like to fill our heads with empty promises and a lot of BS. We are important, and we can and do make a difference. We work hard, our families matter. Legislators pass ridiculous laws saying we can't sue because our employers have these Workers' Compensation policies. What good does a Workers' Compensation policy do if all of the injured workers' injuries are not taken care of under that policy? What good is Workers' Compensation if the insurance company delays and denies treatment? What good is a Workers' Compensation commission if they don't enforce the laws? Letting the insurance companies get out of paying is not right. States need to take a good hard look at these unfair, discriminatory laws and make a change, protecting injured workers in every single state should be the priority.

Chapter 23

One day in August, I went to see my mom, and she said, "I have this hard, painful knot in my breast." I said, "Let me see."

My mom showed me, and I felt it. It was hard as a rock and quite large. I asked her, "Mom, how long has that been there?" She replied, "I don't know, I just noticed it."

I was worried and immediately called her doctor, but they couldn't get her in. So, I took my mom to urgent care, and I accompanied her during the visit. The doctor examined her and said, "This is not good. I'm going to call the hospital and have a mammogram set up right away. We'll have to wait for the mammogram results, but I'm concerned." I asked if it could be cancer, and she replied, "That is a possibility."

The hospital called the same day and scheduled a mammogram for the next morning. My mom had just turned 82 years old, and this was her first mammogram. After the mammogram, we were informed that the results would be sent to the doctor. We hadn't even made it home when the doctor called; it was cancer in both breasts. It was heartbreaking news, especially considering my dad had four sisters, my aunts, who all died from breast cancer.

I had started getting mammograms at the age of twenty-seven and had always tried to persuade my mom to get one as well, but she had resisted. I cannot stress enough how important it is for women to get their yearly mammograms; early detection is key.

Her doctor scheduled an appointment at the breast cancer center for later that week. We attended that appointment, and they scheduled another appointment with a surgeon to determine the next steps. We quickly got in to see the surgeon, who informed us that the cancer in the left breast was large and had been there for a while, while the right one was of medium size. They recommended a double mastectomy.

The surgery was scheduled for the following week, and my mom would undergo a biopsy of a couple of lymph nodes before the surgery to check for any spread. Accompanying my mom to these appointments was challenging, as we had to arrive at least an hour ahead of time to convince her to come along. She would often start arguments, and we never knew if it would be a good or bad day.

She began making unfounded accusations, claiming that her landlord was sneaking in and stealing her belongings or tampering with her food. Her landlord had always been a pleasant person, and such claims were baseless. My mom also insisted that she never watched her TV and offered it to me. After taking it home, she accused me of stealing it just two days later, despite her initial offer. I brought it back as she demanded.

My mom would often help others, whether it was her kids or grandkids, and if she had something, she would give it to them. However, her dementia was worsening, and she started accusing people of attempting to poison her food, leading to her throwing away perfectly good meals. She would forget what food she had bought and buy more of the same items. At one point, she had ten boxes of fish sticks, and when I pointed it out, she got angry and berated me for telling her what to do.

There were instances when a light bulb went out, and we bought replacements, only for her to want to go buy more the very next day. If we told her she didn't need them, it would lead to a heated argument and verbal abuse. The following month, my mom had the double mastectomy. When she woke up from the surgery, she was upset and calling for me.

During her hospital stay, a nurse asked if my mom had memory impairment, and I mentioned that I believed she had dementia. The nurse agreed with my assessment. Before the double mastectomy, they took a biopsy of her lymph nodes, and we were informed that we would receive the results in a couple of weeks.

After coming home, my mom stayed with us for a few days, but she had trouble leaving her bandages alone. She had a vacuum bandage that was meant to expedite healing but kept picking at it, requiring it to be resealed and vacuumed three times while in the hospital. She was resistant to staying with us, preferring to be on her own. However, she was unable to leave her bandage alone, leading to a call to a home nurse to redo it.

Finally, her appointment to remove the drains arrived. By then, the biopsy results were in, and it was revealed that the cancer had spread to the lymph nodes. We were directed to the local cancer center, not the one my daughter had visited.

The doctor informed us that it was an aggressive type of cancer, and I conveyed this to my mom. She responded, "If I had known it was in my lymph nodes, I would have kept my breasts." I believe they should conduct the biopsy before performing a double mastectomy, allowing the individual to make an informed choice.

The doctor suggested additional surgery, but my mom firmly declined. He then said, "You have about a year, give or take. We should start chemotherapy right away." My mom's response was a resolute "NO." The doctor persisted, suggesting, "At least take the chemo pill," but my mom again refused. He finally remarked, "Well, at her age, I guess it doesn't matter." I felt compelled to point out that his comment was rude.

The doctor also advised her to watch her diet, avoiding sweets and soda. I countered that if she only had a year, she could eat whatever she wanted. This cancer center was unlike the one my daughter had visited; it was marked by rudeness, long wait times, and apparent indifference.

I suggested we go to the cancer center my daughter frequented, which was known for its kindness and care. However, my mom swiftly cut me off with a firm "NO," stating that she didn't want to spend her remaining time feeling sick.

A couple of months passed, and my mom had another check-up with the surgeon. He examined the site where her breast had been removed, and it appeared to be healing well. However, when he mentioned her cancer, she made a dismissive gesture and pointed to her ear in a circular motion, signaling her belief that he was talking nonsense. I admonished her for her rudeness.

In the car, she expressed her frustration, calling the doctor stupid and questioning why he was discussing cancer when she had already had her breast removed. I explained that the cancer had spread to her lymph nodes, but that only fueled her anger. She accused me of lying and swore that she wouldn't go anywhere with me again.

Throughout the journey home, she hurled insults and curses at me, even physically striking me at one point while I was driving. I chose to remain silent, not wanting to escalate the situation. Upon arriving at her house, I decided that we wouldn't discuss her cancer anymore, hoping that she might forget about it by the next day.

As I left, she directed obscene gestures and insults toward me, demanding that I never return. Some days, I felt utterly drained, wondering how I would endure another day. My life seemed to be unraveling, and I cried in despair. I questioned why our family had to bear so much hardship.

Tracy's condition wasn't improving, my daughter had mast cell disease, my son had a heart condition, and now my mom not only had cancer but also dementia, which was transforming her into a stranger. I wondered how much more I could endure and prayed for strength to navigate these challenges.

I pleaded with God for guidance and assistance, as the toll of dementia was not only difficult for the person experiencing it but also for their loved ones. It erases the person you once knew, leaving only a hollow shell behind. Where was the mom I used to know? I begged her to come back to me.

Losing my dad when I was twenty-four was already a significant hardship, and now I was witnessing my mom's gradual disappearance each day. It was an incredibly tough period in my life.

Chapter 24

During the second week of December, Tracy's Workers' Compensation check didn't arrive. Initially, I thought it was just delayed, but as another week passed without a check, I grew concerned. Two checks were now overdue. Tracy contacted his attorney, who suggested that the delay might be due to the holiday season and increased mail traffic.

I visited a Workers' Compensation group online and discovered that many people were experiencing the same issue – they hadn't received their checks either. These individuals had various insurance carriers, indicating that it wasn't isolated to one company. Single parents shared stories of needing the checks for essentials like food, bills, rent, and even buying Christmas presents for their children. My husband was also in need of his check.

Week three arrived, and still, no checks had arrived. Tracy tried calling his attorney, but received a message stating that she

Crushed Dreams: A Workers' Compensation Nightmare

would be out of the office until after New Year's. It was frustrating not to have received any checks for three weeks.

After New Year's, all three checks finally arrived, all with the same postmark, indicating they were mailed after New Year's. It became evident that the delay wasn't due to Christmas mail; the checks simply hadn't been sent out.

Returning to the Workers' Compensation group, I found that others had experienced the same delay, receiving their checks after New Year's. I decided to contact a representative and share our experience. His response was disheartening. He mentioned that insurance companies sometimes employ such tactics to motivate injured workers to return to work by creating financial hardship for them and their families.

This approach puts stress on injured workers and their families as they struggle to pay bills, buy food, and meet other essential needs. It's saddening that some believe this tactic is acceptable. In reality, it seems that Workers' Compensation takes advantage of injured workers rather than the other way around. If a doctor has deemed a person unfit for work, it's likely because they cannot work at the moment. People rely on these checks for necessities.

Withholding checks to pressure individuals to return to work before they're fully healed is unfair. This practice doesn't just hurt injured workers; it also impacts their dependents, including children who may have to go without due to delayed payments. It's distressing that insurance companies employ such tactics, and even more troubling that some representatives consider it acceptable to burden families in this way.

These are real challenges faced by people on Workers' Compensation, and it's important to shed light on these issues.

In January 2021, Tracy was presented with the option of getting a spinal cord stimulator to manage his pain. However, before proceeding with this treatment, a psychological evaluation was required. Tracy attended the psychological evaluation and was approved for the procedure.

On January 29, 2021, he underwent a trial spinal cord stimulator implant, which was later removed a few days afterward. The trial had been successful, leading to plans for the permanent spinal cord stimulator.

Come March 25, 2021, Tracy went in for the permanent spinal cord stimulator implant. Due to COVID-19 restrictions, I had to wait in the car as they weren't allowing anyone to accompany patients inside. The surgery was expected to last two and a half to three hours.

However, an hour into the surgery, I received a call informing me to come inside as complications had arisen. The doctor explained that she had to halt the surgery because, upon examination, Tracy's condition was more complex than initially anticipated. There was extensive damage from previous injuries, making the procedure too challenging to complete. As a result, we needed to find a different neurosurgeon with expertise in complex cases.

In the meantime, Tracy was in severe pain after the surgery, exacerbated by his Complex Regional Pain Syndrome (CRPS), which flared up whenever he underwent surgery. A CRPS flare-up causes excruciating pain, burning sensations, temperature sensitivities, and extreme discomfort, making post-surgery recovery particularly difficult.

During this period, Tracy also experienced hip problems, which made walking painful. Additionally, he had a lump the size of a golf ball in his left buttock for two and a half years, causing discomfort when sitting or lying down. We sought the expertise of another orthopedic surgeon.

Our youngest daughter had been planning her wedding for April 2021, and it was rapidly approaching. She and her fiancé were also expecting a baby in September 2021. Despite the challenges, her wedding day turned out beautifully, and our family celebrated the joyous occasion. Tracy's uncle George fell ill during this time, which led to hospitalization after a shower accident. His condition deteriorated, and he was transferred to another hospital.

Tracy had an orthopedic appointment on April 14, 2021, which included X-rays and an MRI. He was scheduled for a total hip replacement on May 10, 2021. Before the surgery, there were pre-testing and hip replacement classes on May 5, 2021. Due to our distance from the hospital, we stayed in a hotel the night before the surgery, as the check-in time was 5:00 am.

On the day of the total hip replacement, May 10, 2021, Tracy received anesthesia with the aid of a special disk behind his ear, which prevented him from getting sick after the surgery. This hospital stood out as one of the best we had experienced, with attentive and compassionate nurses in the orthopedic unit. Tracy's orthopedic doctor and nurse were exceptional.

Following the surgery, Tracy shared his relief with the removal of the lump in his buttock, expressing gratitude for the newfound comfort. He had been in pain from this condition for an extended period. Although he experienced some pain from the CRPS flare-up after the surgery, it was less intense than anticipated.

I joined a CRPS support group and learned about the challenges faced by many individuals with CRPS, including lack of support from family and friends. Some people shared stories of their loved ones not understanding the condition, making hurtful comments, or suggesting that they were exaggerating their symptoms. It was disheartening to read about these struggles within the CRPS community.

It's not that easy. My husband used to be a very outgoing person, but now he experiences mood swings depending on the severity of his pain. He often struggles with frustration and gets upset when he can't control the pain. Sometimes, he isolates himself to cope with the burning sensation and avoids anyone touching his skin. Even the slightest touch of clothing on that area bothers him.

Every day, he battles extreme pain, temperature sensitivity, swelling, and difficulty walking. If you have a loved one dealing with CRPS, please try to understand how challenging it is for them to adjust to such a drastic change in their life. My husband simply wishes to reclaim his once-healthy life.

Show compassion because, just like you, they want their life back. People with CRPS need a strong support group, understanding family, and dependable individuals to help them through tough times. They are not lazy or fine; they are grappling with a debilitating nerve disease.

Tracy underwent therapy the day after his hip surgery and immediately noticed a significant improvement in his hip. Stepping and walking felt better. Prior to the surgery, every step he took was excruciatingly painful, and sitting or lying down was unbearable. The removal of the lump was one of the best outcomes.

While his hip may never fully return to its pre-injury state, at least it no longer feels like he's sitting on a golf ball. Tracy continued with physical therapy for the next couple of months, attending sessions three times a week. We were fortunate to find a compassionate physical therapist and an excellent facility, but it required frequent trips to Hot Springs, which is a three-hour drive from our home. The cost of gas for these trips added up quickly.

Chapter 25

In January 2022, our daughter Autumn and her husband were eagerly anticipating the arrival of their baby boy. This marked the addition of two new grandsons, making it a total of five grandchildren in our family. Our blessings were certainly growing.

During this time, my mom's dementia was progressively worsening. I found myself checking on her multiple times a day as she would often wander onto the road. One morning, I went to visit her, calling out her name with no response. I searched her house, growing increasingly worried. Eventually, I found her curled up on the floor in a fetal position. She was unable to answer me at first, and I called for an ambulance.

As she slowly began to regain her faculties, she asked when she had fallen, clearly disoriented and confused. She even questioned my identity, asking if I could call her daughter Donna, to which I replied, "I'm Donna." It was a heartbreaking and bewildering moment.

Mom had injured her leg and was transported to the hospital. Over the following days, I discussed the situation with hospital staff, explaining that my husband was also dealing with health issues, requiring my constant attention and transportation to various appointments. Meanwhile, my mom's dementia was worsening.

After consulting with the doctors, it became evident that my mom needed more supervision and care than I could provide. Faced with a difficult decision, and with our packed schedule of appointments, I had no choice but to find a nursing home for her. It was a decision I never wanted to make, but circumstances had cornered me.

We located a nursing home an hour away that was willing to accept my mom, mainly because she had tested positive for COVID upon arriving at the hospital. Once she recovered from COVID, I could finally visit her. I made the trip to see her 3-4 times a week.

Meanwhile, Tracy's uncle remained in the hospital from May through June and was released on July 4th. I accompanied Aunt Ann to pick up Uncle George, and the month of July brought another challenge.

I received a call from the nursing home informing me that my mom was attempting to leave, emphasizing the need to find a nursing home with a dementia ward. I managed to locate a facility closer to our home, just 30 minutes away, which had a locked dementia ward. This provided better security for her, as she would no longer be able to wander off.

During our visits, Mom would sometimes mention being at the bus station and needing me to pick her up. Some days, she wouldn't recognize me at all, insisting that she hadn't seen her daughter in months. The proximity of the new nursing home made it easier to visit her.

ne particularly distressing incident involved her claiming her daughter had been kidnapped shortly after my visit. When she called me in a panic, I assured her that I was fine and had just been with her. She questioned why I had left her at the bus station. It was heartbreaking to witness the progression of her dementia, and at times, it was challenging to find the right words to say.

Chapter 26

Tracy continued his visits to pain management, and in July, he began seeing a new neurosurgeon for his back issues. During his first appointment, the neurosurgeon reviewed his medical records and ordered a new MRI for his back. After carefully examining the MRI and his records, the neurosurgeon expressed confidence in performing the surgery. In August, a surgery date was scheduled.

During this time, Tracy's uncle's health took a turn for the worse. Just a few days after returning home, his condition deteriorated significantly. His aunt called for assistance, and both my son and I rushed over to her house. Seeing how bad he was, we immediately drove him to the hospital. He was unresponsive during the ride, and I had to use my flashers to get there quickly. At our local hospital, they informed us that he would need to be transferred to the VA hospital. Uncle George had served in the army for many years, and we were grateful for the sacrifices made by all the men and women who serve our country to protect our freedom.

Crushed Dreams: A Workers' Compensation Nightmare

Uncle George's condition didn't improve at the hospital; in fact, he gradually worsened. Many people offered prayers and support for him during this challenging time.

In August, we celebrated my mom's birthday by bringing her a special meal, including fried mushrooms, which she loved. I also got her a delightful small cake shaped like a dog from a local bakery, as well as a happy birthday balloon from the dollar store and her favorite perfume. She seemed pleased with the surprise. However, when I asked if she wanted to share the cake, she declined. Returning a couple of days later, I found the cake untouched on her nightstand. Strangely, she couldn't remember our previous visit and believed it was her birthday because of the balloon and cake. When I clarified that I had brought the cake two days ago, she became upset, insisting that she didn't like chocolate cake. I reminded her it was a white cake, and she grew angry, calling me names and demanding I take the cake with me and never return. This unpredictability is the nature of dementia; visits can be unpredictable, and each one is different.

My heart goes out to those who have loved ones dealing with dementia. August 2021 marked Tracy's successful surgery for the permanent spinal cord stimulator. However, when we tried to leave, the car wouldn't start. I had forgotten to turn off the lights, and it had drained the battery. We called for assistance, and after a jumpstart, we headed home. Tracy experienced excruciating pain due to a flare-up with his CRPS from the surgery, which was even worse than his usual CRPS pain. He also suffered from post-operative pain. Tracy had endured so much over the last three years, far more than anyone should ever have to go through.

Uncle George showed no signs of improvement; he was on a ventilator, and visitation was restricted due to the severity of COVID in the hospital. Our daughter, who was due in September, developed pre-eclampsia, requiring close monitoring for both her and the baby. With so much happening in our lives, this period was emotionally exhausting and painful. We prayed for Tracy's health, our daughter and grandson's well-being, Uncle George and Aunt Ann, and my mom. The emotional toll was immense.

Tracy's knee remained unstable after his initial total knee replacement, so we consulted the same orthopedic doctor who had performed his total hip replacement. Tracy had been using a cane for quite some time, and he described how his knee wasn't improving; it remained unstable and incredibly painful. At times, his knee would unexpectedly buckle, causing him to fall.

The orthopedic doctor conducted X-rays and confirmed that the knee was indeed loose, with a visible gap evident in the X-ray. He recommended a knee revision surgery to address the issue, and Tracy's surgery was scheduled for September.

The last few weeks of August were exceptionally challenging for us. Our daughter, who was expecting a baby named Colton in January, faced complications due to preeclampsia. She had to undergo monitoring and received shots to strengthen the baby's lungs, preparing for a potentially early delivery. We monitored her closely, aiming for her to reach 37 weeks of pregnancy.

Meanwhile, Uncle George's health deteriorated further, and it was evident that he wasn't improving. The situation became even more difficult when hospital staff recommended taking him off the ventilator. Aunt Ann, his wife, disagreed and wanted to provide him with comfort and support at home in his final days. She initially created a list of family members to be allowed in during his last days.

However, the hospital ultimately decided to restrict access to only immediate family members, despite Uncle George and Aunt Ann not having children of their own. This decision was heartbreaking, as it prevented other nieces and nephews, who were close to Uncle George, from saying their goodbyes. We advocated for Uncle George and contacted a state representative, as well as hospital administrators, expressing our frustration with the situation. We reminded them that Uncle George had served his country and deserved better treatment in his final days.

As time was running out and Uncle George's condition was deteriorating rapidly, we pleaded for the opportunity for family members to visit. Eventually, we received a call allowing Tracy and me to see Uncle George on the evening of September 1, 2021. We rushed to the hospital, and even though Uncle George was heavily sedated and his heart rate had dropped significantly, we sang songs and talked to him, providing comfort in his final moments. He touched my arm when I sang "Amazing Grace," and his heart rate increased briefly. We assured him that it wasn't a goodbye but a "see you later." We also shared our faith and the hope of reuniting in the afterlife. It was a deeply emotional and poignant moment.

Sadly, during the COVID pandemic, many individuals, including veterans, were kept away from their loved ones during their final moments in the hospital. This was a deeply unjust situation. We returned home, but in the early hours of September 2,

2021, we received the news that Uncle George had passed away, finding solace in the knowledge that he had gone home to be with our Lord and Savior.

Soon after, we experienced both sorrow and joy as our daughter reached 37 weeks of pregnancy, and labor was induced. I was at the hospital with her during her labor, simultaneously writing Uncle George's obituary. It was a bittersweet day filled with the sadness of losing a loved one and the happiness of welcoming a new family member into the world.

Our daughter endured a long labor, lasting 36 hours, which ultimately led to an emergency c-section. Baby Colton was born, and although he appeared rough due to the prolonged labor, we were overjoyed that both our grandsons were now safe and sound.

Uncle George received a military funeral, with the Arkansas honor guard doing an exceptional job. We bid farewell to a good man, deeply saddened by his passing but grateful for the time we had with him. He would be sorely missed.

Chapter 27

In late September, Tracy underwent pretesting for his knee and was subsequently scheduled for a revision of his total knee replacement. We made the trip to Hot Springs the night before the surgery, with Tracy being the second surgery on the schedule. Unfortunately, his surgery had to be canceled due to complications with the previous surgery.

This turn of events left us disappointed and financially strained, as we had incurred hotel expenses with no surgery performed. Thankfully, the surgery was rescheduled for two weeks later in October, and this time, the doctor ensured that Tracy would be the first surgery of the day. We returned to Hot Springs, spending the night in a hotel before arriving at the hospital at 5:00 am.

The hospital staff were once again very accommodating, and Tracy was given a special device behind his ear to prevent post-anesthesia sickness. Remarkably, Tracy did not experience any nausea after the surgery, marking another successful surgery without complications.

Following the surgery, the doctor spoke to me and explained that he had discovered significant issues with the initial total knee replacement. Behind Tracy's knee, ligaments had been left hanging, and the doctor had to clean up this mess. Additionally, he had to double the size of the implant to ensure stability.

After Tracy emerged from recovery, the doctor spoke to him directly and reiterated the details of the surgery. It became evident that the previous surgeon had used the wrong implant size and had neglected to address Tracy's complaints of pain and instability following the initial knee replacement.

Tracy had suffered through an excruciating first total knee replacement, and this revision surgery was equally painful. It was followed by more rounds of physical therapy. Additionally, each surgery triggered severe flare-ups of his Complex Regional Pain Syndrome (CRPS), resulting in two to three weeks of intense pain.

To recap Tracy's medical journey so far: he had undergone hip surgery, knee surgery, spent six months in a wheelchair before transitioning to a walker and then a cane. He had a trial spinal cord surgery, followed by a failed permanent spinal cord stimulator surgery, and finally a successful permanent spinal cord stimulator surgery. Months of physical therapy, ongoing pain management, multiple hip and lumbar injections, back ablation, a total knee replacement, and a total hip replacement had all been part of his challenging path. Tracy had also been diagnosed with CRPS, a debilitating nerve disease.

Moreover, with a spinal cord stimulator in place, he would require future surgeries to replace the battery and monitor the unit. Thus, ongoing care for the spinal cord stimulator was necessary.

As November approached, we prepared for a baby shower to welcome baby Ollie into our family. In late November, Tracy had a follow-up appointment with the orthopedic doctor, which led to more scheduled physical therapy sessions as part of his continued recovery.

In December 2021, we received a wonderful Christmas present: baby Oliver had arrived, a delightful addition to our daughter Autumn and her husband Alec, along with their big brother Asher. Their small family was a true blessing.

Moving into January 2022, more physical therapy was prescribed, extending for another six weeks. In February, there was a neurologist appointment for checking and adjusting Tracy's spinal cord stimulator. This time, we saw a new doctor, as the previous neurosurgeon had retired.

The entire journey since the accident had been an exhausting mental roller coaster, marked by emotional and physical pain, as well as an overwhelming financial struggle. After a long legal battle, Workers' Compensation finally accepted the back injury in 2022. However, the judge ruled that they wouldn't have to cover any expenses related to pain management for the back, nor would they pay for neurosurgeon or neurologist appointments concerning the back, the three back surgeries, or any of the thousands of miles traveled to seek treatment. This ruling stemmed from the fact that during the three years when they denied the back injury, they expected individuals like Tracy to sit idly and wait for them to acknowledge the documented injury, effectively deeming any treatment received as "unauthorized treatment."

Tracy's attorney assured us that these expenses would eventually be covered, but this approach didn't align with our understanding. Workers' Compensation seemed to take advantage of their ability to deny coverage by waiting to accept an injury until after all treatments were completed. This practice, we believed, was a tactic employed to avoid paying on the claim. It shouldn't be permitted, and it doesn't protect the injured worker. Insurance companies should face significant fines when they deny a documented injury and refuse to pay for related treatments. Unfortunately, these tactics and loopholes persist, and it's high time they were eliminated.

We should all question when enough people will be outraged by the mistreatment of injured workers and demand that existing laws are enforced. For Tracy, after four long years, the back injury was finally accepted, but this acceptance was of little value, as they had managed to avoid covering the expenses related to the injury.

Furthermore, it took three years to receive the owed compensation from October 2019 to December 2019. They also evaded reimbursing us for the mileage we had to pay out of pocket to attend appointments, despite the law requiring such reimbursement. Passing laws that promise reimbursement for mileage but allowing insurance companies to find ways around it is counterproductive.

The Governor, the House of Representatives, state senators, state congressmen, and business owners who pay high Workers' Compensation insurance premiums should all be concerned that employees are not receiving proper care when injured on the job. These employers are paying for insurance with the expectation that their employees will be taken care of, but that is not always the case. The Workers' Compensation commission must ensure that the laws are enforced and that insurance companies cannot deny legitimate claims to evade payment.

Lastly, the Workers' Compensation judges who rule in favor of insurance companies should reevaluate the laws and ensure that they are upheld. Where is the justice for injured workers, and when will their rights be protected? These questions must be addressed, and the voices of injured workers need to be heard.

The prolonged struggle took a toll on me mentally, emotionally, and physically, leaving me drained and weary.

I used to visit my mom at the nursing home three to four times a week. Her dementia was worsening, and during her phone calls from the nursing home, she'd make distressing claims, like the police having her or being at work with no one to pick her up. She even mentioned being stuck at a bus station without being allowed on the bus. Witnessing her in this state was incredibly tough.

Moreover, it was heartbreaking to see many other dementia patients suffering similarly, as I had grown acquainted with some of them through my visits to my mom. What saddened me was the number of individuals in nursing homes who didn't receive any visitors.

I noticed that many female patients had baby dolls, which sparked an idea. I asked the nurses if I could bring in some gently used stuffed animals or baby dolls, and they enthusiastically agreed. My granddaughters had an excess of toys that needed to be cleared out, so I decided to clean them up and bring them in. I washed the stuffed animals, added new ribbons to them, and spruced up the baby dolls with fresh outfits.

The impact of these small gestures was profound. The residents at the nursing home found immense joy in these simple gifts. If you happen to have stuffed animals or baby dolls that you're considering donating to a thrift store, I encourage you to wash them up and drop them off at your local nursing home for the residents. It's a small act of kindness that can bring immense joy and comfort to those in need.

Chapter 28

Tracy's right shoulder was causing him a lot of pain, and his right knee had started to trouble him as well, causing both discomfort and difficulties in walking. During a visit to his orthopedic doctor, the physician observed an abnormal gait in Tracy's walk. The doctor pointed out that Tracy was unintentionally shifting his weight to his right side, a common response to reduce discomfort in an injured area. Even though Tracy was using a cane for almost three years, it had begun to take a toll on his shoulder. Before the revision surgery on his left knee, Tracy was highly unstable on his feet and had experienced several falls due to his knee giving way, often resulting in hard impacts on his right shoulder.

The journey since the accident had been arduous, leaving lasting effects on Tracy's body. His CRPS appeared to be spreading, compounding the physical challenges he faced. The initial orthopedic doctor conducted X-rays of both knees and reported that the right knee appeared healthy in 2019. However, the accident had set off a chain reaction in Tracy's body, transforming him from a fit, active individual into someone with the body of an 80-year-old. This accident had taken a significant toll on him, not just physically, but mentally, emotionally, and financially.

Going from a workaholic who put in over 55 hours a week to living a life filled with pain, doctor appointments, surgeries, physical therapy, and a debilitating nerve disease had been an immense adjustment. Previously, Tracy and his partner enjoyed an active life filled with outdoor activities like walking trails, climbing Sugar Loaf Mountain, jet skiing, and tubing. However, all of that had changed, forcing them to adapt to a more sedentary lifestyle. This shift had also impacted their intimacy, adding to the challenges they faced as a couple.

Their journey had made them realize the importance of the marriage vows they took, particularly the commitment to being there for each other in times of adversity. They had started their journey feeling invincible, but the accident had tested their relationship in unimaginable ways. Despite the difficulties, they cherished every moment together, even though CRPS was considered one of the most painful diseases.

Witnessing Tracy's daily battle with excruciating pain was heartbreaking and emotionally overwhelming. It was a struggle they faced together, and unless someone experienced it firsthand, they couldn't truly understand the extent of the pain. The author expressed heartfelt empathy for all individuals living with CRPS, recognizing the unimaginable suffering they endured.

Tracy had often expressed his love for his family but also his uncertainty about whether it would be enough to keep him going. He questioned his strength to endure the relentless pain day after day, praying for the strength to make it through each day. The uncertainty of what the future held made it difficult for him to look too far ahead, as he couldn't predict what each new day would bring. Despite it all, he was grateful for making it through each hard, painful day.

The author reflected on how they never could have imagined that the person they loved would endure such pain and have such a broken body. It was a frightening reality, as CRPS was often referred to as the "suicide disease" due to the unbearable pain it caused. While the author didn't experience the daily pain firsthand, she witnessed Tracy's struggles, his restless nights, and his moaning in pain during the few hours of sleep he managed to get. It was a painful journey for both of them.

The author also grappled with anger, particularly towards the person who had caused her husband's injury. She found it profoundly unjust that if the injury had occurred anywhere else, the responsible party would have faced legal consequences. However, because it happened at work, there were no repercussions for the actions that had led to Tracy's suffering. She also harbored anger towards Tracy's employer for their treatment of him after the accident. Over time, she recognized that forgiveness was essential for her own peace of mind. Letting go of this anger was challenging, but it ultimately lifted a heavy burden, bringing a sense of relief and allowing her to move forward.

In conclusion, the author acknowledged the difficulties they had faced over the past few years but emphasized the importance of forgiveness for finding inner peace. The journey had been

Crushed Dreams: A Workers' Compensation Nightmare

tough, but it had also strengthened their bond, teaching them the value of their commitment to one another in both good times and bad.

Chapter 29

Over the months, my mom's dementia deteriorated significantly. She could recall fragments of events from long ago, but her short-term memory had completely vanished. She struggled to differentiate between people who visited her, often expressing disappointment, saying, "Why don't you come to see me?" despite my frequent visits, which occurred three to four times a week. Her cancer had taken a toll on her fragile, frail body, causing her muscles to weaken. She had gone from being able to walk independently to relying on a walker, and eventually, a wheelchair full-time.

In addition to her memory loss, she could no longer control her bladder and bowels, and she was losing weight rapidly. Her congestive heart problems were worsening, and there were moments when we feared she might not make it. During these trying times, I turned to prayer for my mom.

I prayed for God's will to be done, asking Heavenly Father to heal her body and mind if it was His will. However, I also prayed that if healing was not in His plan, He would spare her from unnecessary suffering. Losing my mom was a prospect I couldn't bear, but I also couldn't bear to see her endure such pain.

Momma experienced a great deal of fluid accumulation in her legs, often expressing how much pain she was in. She struggled to breathe, and it was heart-wrenching to witness her body wasting away while her mind deteriorated.

In December of 2020, the doctor had given us the prognosis that she had roughly a year left to live. Momma had a fondness for Mt. Dew, and whenever she felt particularly unwell, she would ask for it. A can of Mt. Dew seemed to provide her with a brief pick-me-up during those moments. Our family humorously referred to it as "grandma's cure."

She had become reliant on oxygen full-time, and sometimes, the kids or grandkids would accompany me when visiting her. Occasionally, I would take her out of the nursing home to run errands or attend events, like the drive-through Christmas lights in town, which she thoroughly enjoyed. These were the moments I cherished, creating lasting memories with her.

Our family had faced immense challenges over the last four years, but we held onto the precious moments and memories we were creating with momma during this difficult journey.

Chapter 30

Tracy continued to experience issues with his right shoulder, prompting his Orthopedic doctor to advise, "You have to try to get off that cane." Leaning on the cane to alleviate the pressure when he walked didn't help; he had experienced too many falls due to the instability of his knee and hip, and now his right knee was causing problems as well.

In addition to Tracy's health concerns, my father-in-law, who had suffered a major stroke in 2017, was showing worrisome signs of illness and frequent falls. We suspected he might be having mini-strokes, so his doctor referred him to a cardiologist to ensure his heart was in good condition before consulting a neurologist. This led to numerous doctor visits and hospital trips for my father-in-law.

In May, we received the exciting news of another grandchild on the way. It would be the second baby for our daughter

Crushed Dreams: A Workers' Compensation Nightmare

Alicia and her husband Colby, completing their family. While they were most hopeful for a healthy baby, they were also excited about the possibility of a baby sister for their firstborn.

In June 2022, Tracy underwent shoulder surgery due to severe pain and limited arm movement. After the surgery, he couldn't use his cane, making walking painful and less appealing. Tracy's life in recent years seemed to revolve around doctor appointments, surgeries, and physical therapy.

August brought a gender reveal, announcing a baby brother on the way. My daughter was going to be a "boy mom," and baby Trace was set to join our family in January 2023. It was an exciting time for our growing family, bringing much-needed joy to our lives.

Meanwhile, my father-in-law's condition worsened. He was diagnosed with a brain tumor, and attempts to remove it through surgery were unsuccessful. His prognosis was grim, and he entered hospice care. My husband's step-dad, as his biological father had passed away when he was just 16, had a large family with 18 siblings from the same parents. Some of his siblings from out of state visited, and we gathered for a bonfire and a big BBQ dinner, sharing laughter and reminiscing about good times.

As the weekend of celebration came to an end, his siblings bid their farewells and returned home. Within two days, my father-in-law's health took a rapid decline, and he slipped into a morphine coma. He passed away on a Thursday in October, finding relief from suffering and joining the Lord. It was a somber moment, witnessing the departure of loved ones.

Over the last four years, we had witnessed so much sickness and had to say goodbye to two cherished family members.

Chapter 31

In October 2022, Tracy was invited to speak at a SAFETY conference organized by the Department of Labor. During his presentation, he showcased a slide show of his injuries, and on stage, there were empty chairs symbolizing each person who had tragically lost their life while on the job in Arkansas.

Seeing those empty chairs had a profound impact. The statistics were sobering:

- 2018 witnessed 76 fatalities.

- 2019 had 62 fatalities.

- 2020 recorded 64 fatalities.

- 2021 reported 74 fatalities.

Every empty chair represented a life lost, leaving behind grieving families. These numbers were just for one state, and the nationwide toll of workplace injuries and deaths was even more staggering. Tracy's story highlighted the challenges of navigating Workers' Compensation, but for many families, their loved ones never return home from work, and accidents that could have been prevented lead to lifelong consequences.

The message was clear: safety rules must be followed diligently on the job. The lives of workers and their colleagues depend on it. Everyone goes to work hoping to return home in the same good health they left with.

In November, we celebrated with a baby shower for our daughter. December brought unexpected challenges as she experienced pre-eclampsia once again. Baby Trace wasn't going to wait until January; it seemed he would make a December entrance. Alicia received shots to strengthen his lungs at 35 weeks, and by 36 weeks, they couldn't wait any longer. Baby Trace arrived shortly after Christmas, becoming the second December grandson, following baby Ollie's birth the previous December. Alicia, her husband Colby, their son Colton, and now baby Trace completed their beautiful family of four.

In January 2023, Tracy continued to have appointments with the orthopedic doctor as his right knee began causing problems. Despite initially appearing healthy on x-rays, the years of shifting his weight to the right side had taken a toll on what was once considered his "good knee." The doctor had compared the injured knee to the uninjured one, pointing out the stark differences and how the left knee should have looked. Now, Tracy had no good knees. After five years, he faced yet another surgery, and it seemed that his once-healthy body had only deteriorated since his injury. The toll of heavy equipment versus the human body had left him in constant pain with no relief in sight.

We made another trip to Hot Springs, staying overnight, and Tracy had to be at the hospital by 5:00 am. At the hospital, they administered a disk behind his ear to alleviate anesthesia-induced nausea. We prayed together, and he went into surgery.

The doctor came to see me after the surgery and said, "The surgery went well." The nurses at this hospital are always incredibly kind and nice, and they didn't disappoint this time. Tracy mentioned that the pain didn't seem as severe as when he had the other left knee replacement and the revision. He was experiencing a flare-up from the CRPS, but he noted that the actual pain from the total knee replacement was different from when his injured knee had been replaced, which had been absolutely excruciating. He would start physical therapy three times a week for the next six weeks.

In 2008, we purchased a brand new Chrysler Aspen with only 12 miles on it. Equipped with a HEMI engine, it has now accumulated over 400,000 miles. We diligently performed all scheduled maintenance, including oil changes every 3,000 miles, throughout the lifetime of this vehicle. Without proper maintenance, it would never have reached 400,000 miles.

The Lifetime Powertrain Warranty covers the cost of all parts and labor needed to repair covered powertrain components, including the engine, transmission, and drive system. However, the new powertrain warranty is limited to the first registered owner, and it requires an inspection every five years to remain valid. We took our Aspen in for a recall in 2013, where I believe

Crushed Dreams: A Workers' Compensation Nightmare

they conducted the required inspection. Unfortunately, we were unaware of the need for these inspections. It appears that we were supposed to have one in 2018, but given the events of that year, it's understandable that we wouldn't have remembered. Such clauses are often designed to be easily forgotten.

When I contacted Chrysler about this issue, they congratulated us on having the Aspen with the most miles. It's worth noting that the vehicle reached this milestone due to proper maintenance. However, I found numerous other Chrysler owners who, like us, had faithfully maintained their vehicles and were upset that Chrysler was not honoring the lifetime powertrain warranty. Furthermore, I learned that a person, along with twenty-seven other owners, had filed a class-action lawsuit against Chrysler for not honoring the warranty. Every original owner who experienced this should be part of that lawsuit.

Chrysler advertised the powertrain warranty as one of the reasons we purchased the Aspen brand new. Our transmission is still functioning well after over 400,000 miles. If companies are not going to honor their promotions, perhaps they should reconsider running them altogether. Promotions attract buyers, but when they include hidden clauses in small print (often called "mouse print") that most people are unaware of, it becomes a way for companies to avoid honoring warranties. I, for one, will never buy from a company that fails to honor its warranty commitments. Making it to over 400,000 miles on an engine is a testament to proper maintenance, and my experienced mechanic husband has done an excellent job taking care of the vehicle. No inspection every five years can replace regular maintenance, and it's disappointing that companies sometimes choose not to do the right thing.

Unfortunately, it's a trend where companies often do their best to avoid fulfilling their promises. Thank you, Chrysler, for not replacing the motor as promised, even though we remained the original owners.

Chapter 32

When Tracy got injured, I posted a video on my social media to raise awareness of dangerous accidents like the one that occurred at my husband's workplace. It appears that someone from his company saw the video, as my husband and I both received text messages from unknown sources, likely using a texting app. The text messages read as follows:

Text message #1 was sent to my husband's phone on January 8, 2023: "The videos put on social media need to be removed. It has reached the point of defamation of character and slander. We demand they be removed!"

Firstly, it's important to note that the text message was not signed, and the sender hid behind a texting app. If they wanted their complaint to be taken seriously, they should use their real phone number and identify themselves. Secondly, the video shows my husband getting injured at the company where he worked for

12 years. Slander involves untrue statements or posting something that is untrue. In this case, my husband's injury at the company is a documented fact, and there is nothing untrue about it.

Text message #2 was sent to my phone on February 9, 2023: "I have been patiently waiting for the videos to be removed, and I will be seeking litigation to have the videos removed."

Once again, the sender used a texting app and did not provide their real phone number or identity. If I had done something illegal or made untrue statements, they could involve an attorney. However, it seems that the sender wants the videos removed simply because they reveal the truth. Disliking the truth does not make it slanderous.

Companies should improve their hiring processes and, even after hiring, ensure that employees are capable of performing their job duties. If an employee intentionally harms another employee, the company should promptly report such accidents within the 24-hour timeframe required by OSHA.

I do not know who sent these messages, whether it was someone from the company or not, as they hid behind a texting app. However, it is clear that the sender had both my and my husband's numbers and did not want the truth about his workplace injury to be known. The facts remain that he was injured at his workplace, where he had been employed for 12 years, and another person was responsible for his injury. It is also a fact, confirmed through a letter from OSHA, that the accident was not properly reported. The truth, no matter how unflattering, is not slanderous. Whoever sent these messages, I am not removing the videos as they depict the truth.

I began reaching out to the representative who was introducing the bill he drafted for Workers' Compensation. Finally, 2023 had arrived, and I was hopeful that new laws would be passed, bringing about some real change. However, that hope was short-lived as the representative informed me that the bill he had drafted went nowhere; it had been rejected. I had waited from 2019 until 2023 for some progress, but unfortunately, nothing substantial had materialized. Now, I was told that maybe something could be introduced in 2025. This false hope left me wondering why this wasn't done correctly from the start. Throughout 2019, 2020, 2021, and 2022, the representative should have been aware of how to properly introduce a bill. It was disheartening to think that we would have to wait another two years to try again.

I also spoke with another representative who suggested that an interim study needed to be conducted. This study could be initiated now, not two years down the line. It was frustrating to feel like all the emails, calls, and text messages had gone to waste, especially when the bill never even made it to the representatives for a vote.

In light of these disappointments, I decided to contact the governor and share my husband's story with the hope that she might be willing to help injured workers through an executive order. I filled out an online form to contact the governor, and a few days later, a gentleman from the governor's office called, expressing a desire to meet with us at the capital to discuss my message to the governor. We had a meeting with the governor's Liaison, during which I presented a packet of papers to illustrate my husband's story. While he listened and promised to convey the message to the governor, weeks passed without any follow-up. It felt like another letdown, where listening led to no concrete action.

In March and April, my mom's condition deteriorated further. She had become extremely frail, with weakening muscles, increased disorientation, reduced speech, and a loss of appetite for her favorite foods like fried chicken and fried mushrooms. Surprisingly, she started drinking Mt. Dew, which was unlike her.

On Friday, April 28, 2023, I received a call from the nursing home, informing me that my mom was seriously ill, and I needed to come. When I arrived, I found my mom in excruciating pain. I immediately requested her hospice nurse to be called, but they had already done so. Despite receiving pain medication, she remained in severe pain. I called hospice again, and after several attempts, they increased her dose and left standing orders for the nursing home to adjust it as needed.

Finally, my mom was receiving the right amount of medication to keep her comfortable. I spent the day with her, moistening her mouth with a sponge and singing her favorite songs. My mom eventually slipped into a morphine coma and passed away shortly after midnight on May 1, 2023. Coincidentally, my dad had also passed away shortly after midnight on May 1, 1997. Both succumbed to cancer on the same date.

My mom had bravely fought for nearly three years after being diagnosed, far surpassing the initial prognosis of a year. She was a strong and independent person who gave her all, but cancer and dementia eventually overtook her. She fought valiantly, and her memory will be cherished and missed.

It was a somber period as both of my parents were now gone. My mom had requested no funeral, always saying, "If you can't come and see me while I'm alive, don't come see me after I'm dead." I dressed her in her favorite dress and visited her as she lay at rest. She had also requested no graveside service. Only three of us gathered just before her burial, singing a few of her favorite songs, offering a prayer, and saying our goodbyes.

I arranged for her tombstone, adorned with a beautiful old-time sewing machine, her picture, a needle and thread stitching the word "love" in the corner, a thimble on the last letter of her name, and, of course, a Mt. Dew can, with the inscription: "When life gives you scraps, make a quilt." Mom and Dad were reunited on the other side with our Lord and Savior. Until we meet again, they remain in my heart.

Chapter 33

After my mom passed away, our daughter informed us that she and her husband were about to complete their family, and they had received the news that they would be having a baby girl. After welcoming five grandsons in a row, our eighth grandchild would finally be a girl. We were thrilled about the arrival of our new granddaughter, this special bundle of joy that would complete their beautiful family.

I had taken the initiative to send emails to the Speaker of The House of Representatives in Arkansas and had made several calls to his office. Eventually, I received a response from him, and his message read: "Thank you for your recent call to my office and for your previous emails regarding Workers' Compensation law. I appreciate you sharing your husband's story and your related concerns, and I intend to keep your words in mind for the 2025 legislative session." Instead of representatives merely keeping people's stories in mind, it would be more meaningful if they took concrete actions to make a difference. Real change is needed to assist people, not just contemplation.

After waiting for months to hear back from the governor's office, which never happened, I learned that the Governor was hosting a town hall meeting with a small group of about 200 people in June. I signed up with great excitement and received confirmation that I had been selected. I attended the event, listened to the governor's speech, and afterward, I swiftly moved to get in line. I became the second person in line, and this caught the attention of her security personnel, who kept a watchful eye on me. It was just a piece of paper, nothing to worry about, but in today's world, it's understandable that security is essential.

I had written a heartfelt four-page letter and was eager to personally hand it to the governor, placing it directly in her hands. I politely requested her to read it, explaining that I had put a lot of thought into it. The letter was about the treatment of injured workers in Arkansas, and I hoped that she would consider being a voice for these workers. She responded with a gracious "thank you, I will read it." As I walked away, I felt confident that after she read my letter, I would surely hear from the governor. This time, I had reached out directly to her, eliminating any intermediaries.

I even provided my address and phone number, believing that our compassionate governor would take action to help injured workers. She was already working on initiatives to raise teacher's pay and bring higher-paying jobs to Arkansas. If better, higher-paying jobs come to the state, it makes sense to ensure that highly paid employees receive fair and equal compensation (66%) if they are injured.

However, many weeks passed, and I couldn't wait any longer. I decided to call the state capital to inquire about the governor's response to my letter. They took a message, and the following day, I received a phone call from a staff member of the governor. She said, "She was at that town hall meeting, and the governor received no letter." I was taken aback, as I was the second person in line, and I had personally handed the letter to the governor. I was sure she had received it. I asked what had happened to the letter, and the staff member insisted that the governor had not received it. I offered to email a copy of the letter so that she could ensure it reached the governor personally. She agreed, and I promptly sent a copy of the four-page letter via email. However, to this day, I have not received any response.

It is disheartening that many individuals running for office seem to only care about the people when seeking votes, but once elected, they often forget about those who elected them. I had previously written to the previous governor without receiving any response. I also reached out to both candidates while they were running, and the Democratic nominee never replied. I sent numerous messages, made calls, and left messages with his campaign team, none of which were returned.

I had the opportunity to meet the current governor while she was campaigning, and during our conversation, she expressed compassion for my husband's situation. She told me how fortunate my husband was to have a caring wife. I do care deeply about his well-being, as well as the well-being of all injured workers in Arkansas. I will continue to advocate for awareness and change.

Crushed Dreams: A Workers' Compensation Nightmare

As the first female governor, she has the potential to make a significant impact on behalf of injured workers. I address this message to the Arkansas governor, the four Arkansas congressmen, the Arkansas senators, and all the members of the Arkansas House of Representatives. Arkansas injured workers need each and every one of you to be their voice and advocate for much-needed reform in the state. Arkansas employers must be held accountable when they fail to report accidents to Arkansas OSHA. The state's regulations require employers to report all work-related accidents that result in hospitalization or death, and this crucial requirement needs to be enforced. We all have a role to play in bringing about the necessary changes to Workers' Compensation.

Chapter 34

In September, I came across a person on social media and watched a video posted by her husband. Her name is Kim Frankel, and she hails from Nevada. Kim was a dedicated police officer who was injured on the job when she was rear-ended by a drunk driver. She served as a veteran detective assigned to sex crimes against children, a highly important role.

After her injury, she attempted to return to work, but it soon became evident that her work-related injuries had resulted in a rare neurological condition known as "dystonia." Dystonia is a neurological movement disorder characterized by involuntary (unintended) muscle contractions that lead to slow, repetitive movements or abnormal postures, often causing pain. There are various forms of dystonia that can affect single muscles, groups of muscles, or muscles throughout the body, and the severity and affected areas can vary from person to person.

Crushed Dreams: A Workers' Compensation Nightmare

Despite receiving multiple diagnoses, the county's insurance managers continued to reject her claims. They persisted in denying coverage even after losing their case in court. State Workers' Compensation laws underwent changes in the 1990s that provided little leverage to compel them to act differently. However, Senator Skip Daily introduced SB274, a bill that aimed to address these issues and provide much-needed assistance.

Kim Frankel played a pivotal role in advocating for this bill by testifying and sharing her story with lawmakers. Her compelling testimony and her willingness to be a voice for injured workers brought their issues to the forefront. Thanks to Kim Frankel's bravery and determination to drive change, the bill passed both houses, and the governor of Nevada signed bill SB274 into law in June 2023.

SB274 introduces more transparency into the process, enhances oversight through the commissioner, and imposes stricter penalties for bad faith actions by insurers. Unfortunately, this legislation may not directly benefit Kim Frankel, as the delay in her treatment, now three years past her injury, may have left her with permanent impairment. Many prayers go out to Kim Frankel for her ongoing health and her relentless fight to access the treatment she needs.

People like Kim and myself understand that our efforts may not directly benefit us or our loved ones, but they contribute to the improvement of laws that can help future injured workers receive fair and timely treatment. This is why this book is so important—it sheds light on the challenges faced by injured workers, not only my husband's experiences but those of injured workers across the United States.

    Stories like Kim Frankel's, Scott Pitts', my husband's, and those of countless others who have been treated unfairly, faced delays, or been denied treatment under Workers' Compensation can inspire change. We can make a difference by reaching out to our state representatives and advocating for changes to Workers' Compensation laws, making it fairer for everyone in the workforce. Let's make this call for the sake of the future workforce, our children, and our grandchildren. If we stand by and do nothing, nothing will change. While no one wants to get hurt, the laws should protect those who are.

Crushed Dreams: A Workers' Compensation Nightmare

Chapter 35

In August 2023, after nearly five years of relentless struggle, my husband's case was finally settled. He now has open medical coverage for life for the body parts that were injured. It's a common misconception that people on Workers' Compensation receive substantial settlements, but the reality is quite different. Most individuals simply want their health back, which is often elusive due to delayed or denied treatment—a situation that urgently needs rectification.

Under Workers' Compensation, after a protracted legal battle, they are now obligated to cover any future treatment for his back, hip, or knee. This journey has been long and arduous, and one can't help but wonder what the outcome might have been if OSHA had investigated, if paperwork hadn't been altered, if timely treatment had been provided, and if treatment for the back hadn't been denied for so long.

Crushed Dreams: A Workers' Compensation Nightmare

My husband has now requested Workers' Compensation to start covering his doctor appointments and any other treatment associated with this accident. However, Workers' Compensation insisted on him seeing new doctors. It took over two months to secure an appointment arranged by Workers' Compensation.

This appointment with a new doctor was intended to ensure he had a healthcare provider responsible for his ongoing spinal cord stimulator needs. Despite the case being settled, Workers' Compensation presented this new doctor with questions, such as whether he believed my husband's back had been injured in the work-related accident. This question had already been addressed and substantiated with thousands of pages of medical records, and Workers' Compensation had accepted that outcome.

Another question posed by Workers' Compensation to this new doctor was whether he believed the spinal cord stimulator had been necessary. Neurologists, pain management specialists, neurosurgeons, and even the judge had already ruled on this case, stating that Workers' Compensation should cover any necessary treatment for my husband's back, hip, and knee from this point onward.

Oddly, the new doctor to whom Workers' Compensation sent my husband doesn't even deal with spinal cord stimulators, rendering the appointment less useful. What my husband needed was a doctor to oversee his ongoing treatment for his back, hip, and knee. Despite the judge's ruling, Workers' Compensation continues to be a challenge to work with.

This new doctor spent ten to fifteen minutes with my husband during the initial visit, without reviewing any medical records. Subsequently, he expressed a "medical opinion" that my husband's back was not injured in a work-related accident and that the spinal cord stimulator was "unnecessary." This conclusion was reached despite medical findings in the radiology report that supported a back injury resulting from trauma, such as being crushed.

The audacity of this doctor's opinion, formed after just a brief encounter and without examining medical records, is astounding. He dismissed the assessments of EMTs, ER doctors, family doctors, neurologists, neurosurgeons, pain management specialists, and the multitude of doctors who have treated my husband and documented his medical records.

I reported this doctor to the hospital and the Arkansas Medical Board for attempting to shame my husband for receiving a spinal cord stimulator. Such behavior is unacceptable, and this doctor should be held accountable for attempting to shame people living with chronic pain.

I find it impossible to comprehend the actions of Workers' Compensation insurance companies and doctors. The legislators who vote to uphold this illogical and corrupt system, which fails to protect injured workers, remain equally perplexing. Workers' Compensation can often feel like a never-ending nightmare, persisting even after the judge has ruled on the case.

I'll leave you with these parting words: if you can, please pray for us. If you can help by contacting your state representatives or anyone residing in Arkansas and advocate for better laws, please do so. Call every day, encourage friends and family to make daily calls to their district's representatives, or reach out to the Speaker of the Arkansas House of Representatives. Demand Workers' Compensation reform and the removal of the discriminatory CAP, ensuring that all injured workers receive a fair and equal 66% of their pay if they are injured. Urge the governor to be a voice for injured workers.

    May God bless each person who has taken the time to read our story, and may no one ever have to endure what my husband has gone through. Stay safe in your jobs, and together, we can bring about the much-needed change. One person can raise awareness, and together, we can drive change. Don't give up, injured workers. Keep fighting, and we can all emerge victorious. Together, we can make a difference, because no one should stand alone. Make your voice heard, stay strong, and keep the faith. God bless! We are all important!

www.ingramcontent.com/pod-product-compliance
Lightning Source LLC
Chambersburg PA
CBHW070849050426
42453CB00012B/2110